Mongolia and the United States

ADST-DACOR Diplomats and Diplomacy Series

Series Editor: Margery Boichel Thompson

Since 1776, extraordinary men and women have represented the United States abroad under widely varying circumstances. What they did and how and why they did it remain little known to their compatriots. In 1995, the Association for Diplomatic Studies and Training (ADST) and DACOR, an organization of foreign affairs professionals, created the Diplomats and Diplomacy book series to increase public knowledge and appreciation of the professionalism of American diplomats and their involvement in world history. Ambassador Jonathan Addleton's examination of 25 years of United States–Mongolia diplomatic relations, the 52nd volume in the series, combines history with close-up perspectives on developing ties with an emerging Asian democracy.

Related Titles in the Series

Charles T. Cross, *Born a Foreigner: A Memoir of the American Presence in Asia*

Hermann Frederick Eilts, *Early American Diplomacy in the Near and Far East: The Diplomatic and Personal History of Edmund Q. Roberts (1784–1836)*

John H. Holdridge, *Crossing the Divide: An Insider's Account of Normalization of U.S.-China Relations*

Dennis Kux, *The United States and Pakistan, 1947–2000: Disenchanted Allies*

Terry McNamara, *Escape with Honor: My Last Hours in Vietnam*

William B. Milam, *Bangladesh and Pakistan: Flirting with Failure in Muslim South Asia*

Robert H. Miller, *Vietnam and Beyond: A Diplomat's Cold War Education*

William Michael Morgan, *Pacific Gibraltar: U.S.-Japanese Rivalry over the Annexation of Hawai'i, 1885–1898*

Ronald Neumann, *The Other War: Winning and Losing in Afghanistan*

David D. Newsom, *Witness to a Changing World*

Nicholas Platt, *China Boys: How U.S. Relations with the PRC Began and Grew*

Howard B. Schaffer, *The Limits of Influence: America's Role in Kashmir*

Ulrich Straus, *The Anguish of Surrender: Japanese POWs of World War II*

Nancy Bernkopf Tucker, ed., *China Confidential: American Diplomats and Sino-American Relations, 1945–1996*

Mongolia and the United States

A Diplomatic History

Jonathan S. Addleton

An ADST-DACOR Diplomats and Diplomacy Book

香港大學出版社
HONG KONG UNIVERSITY PRESS

Hong Kong University Press
The University of Hong Kong
Pokfulam Road
Hong Kong
www.hkupress.org

The views and opinions in this book are solely those of the author and not necessarily those of the Association for Diplomatic Studies and Training, DACOR, or the Government of the United States.

ISBN 978-988-8139-94-1 (*Hardback*)

British Library Cataloguing-in-Publication Data
A catalogue record for this book is available from the British Library.

10 9 8 7 6 5 4 3 2 1

Printed and bound by Paramount Printing Co. Ltd., Hong Kong, China

Contents

Acronyms

ABG	American Business Group
ACM	Arts Council of Mongolia
ACMS	American Center for Mongolian Studies
AED	Academy for Educational Development
BCM	Business Council of Mongolia
CEO	Chief Executive Officer
CHF	originally Cooperative Housing Foundation, now just CHF
CNN	Cable News Network
CODEL	Congressional Delegation
DP	Democratic Party
EARC	Educational Advisory and Resource Center
EBRD	European Bank for Reconstruction and Development
ERA	Energy Regulatory Authority
FMF	Foreign Military Financing
GDP	Gross Domestic Product
GDT	General Directorate of Tax
GE	General Electric
GEC	General Election Commission
HDP	House Democracy Partnership
IFC	International Finance Corporation
IMET	International Military Education and Training
IRC	International Rescue Committee
IRI	International Republican Institute
ISAF	International Security Assistance Force

IVLP	International Visitors Leadership Program
KFOR	Kosovo Force
LEND	Leaders Engaged in New Democracies Network
MCA	Millennium Challenge Agency
MCC	Millennium Challenge Corporation
MFAT	Ministry of Foreign Affairs and Trade
MNDP	Mongolian National Democratic Party
MPP	Mongolian People's Party
MPRP	Mongolian People's Revolutionary Party
NAMBC	North American Mongolian Business Council
NATO	North Atlantic Treaty Organization
NCO	Noncommissioned Officer
NCSC	National Center for State Courts
NDI	National Democratic Institute
NEA	Nuclear Energy Agency
NED	National Endowment for Democracy
NEMA	National Emergency Management Agency
NGO	Nongovernmental Organization
NIH	National Institutes of Health
NSF	National Science Foundation
OFDA	Office of Foreign Disaster Assistance
OPIC	Overseas Private Investment Corporation
TDA	Trade Development Agency
TIP	Trafficking in persons
UN	United Nations
UNDP	United Nations Development Program
UPI	United Press International
USAID	United States Agency for International Development
USDA	United States Department of Agriculture
USSR	Union of Soviet Socialist Republics

Glossary of Mongolian Terms

aimag: province

airag: fermented mare's milk

aaruul: traditional Mongolian cheese or dried curd

denj: hill or terrace, as in "American *denj*," the place in Ulaanbaatar where American merchants used to congregate during the early twentieth century

deel: traditional Mongolian dress, worn by both men and women

dzud (or zhud): especially disastrous winter conditions in which herders often lose large numbers of livestock

ger: round felt tent; usually called a "yurt" in English or "yurta" in Russian

Hural: gathering or assembly; the Great Hural is the Mongolian parliament

morin huur: traditional Mongolian stringed instrument, often referred to as the national instrument of Mongolia. The sound it makes is sometimes compared to that of a horse neighing or the wind blowing gently across the steppe.

Naadam: biggest annual festival in Mongolia. It typically takes place in July and includes cultural celebrations and archery, wrestling, and horse racing competitions.

soum: district

soyombo: national symbol of Mongolia, designed by Bogdo Zanabazar in the seventeenth century. It appears on the Mongolian flag.

Tsagaan Sar: the Mongolian lunar new year, usually celebrated in February. It literally means "white moon."

tsam: a Buddhist ritual dance that in Mongolia is performed using elaborate masks

Introduction

On January 27, 1987, senior diplomats from the United States and Mongolia met in a modest ceremony below a portrait of Thomas Jefferson in the Treaty Room of the Department of State in Washington, D.C. Their purpose was to sign the legal documentation needed to finally establish formal diplomatic relations between the two countries. This in turn led to the appointment of the first ambassadors and the opening of new embassies in Ulaanbaatar and Washington. It also became the catalyst for a rapid growth in relations in any number of areas, not only in the political arena but also in culture, education, business, development, and security.

Twenty-five years later, the bilateral relationship between the United States and Mongolia continues to both deepen and expand. In all these areas and more, Mongolians and Americans are increasingly meeting, learning from, understanding, and partnering with each other to achieve common aims and objectives.

This book provides a retrospective look at the first quarter century of diplomatic relations between the United States and Mongolia, recalling in part a dispatch written nearly 100 years ago by an American diplomat named A. W. Ferrin. At the time, Ferrin was a commercial officer assigned to the US legation in "Peking." In his dispatch, he highlighted the growing commercial opportunities available to American businesses in Mongolia. At the same time, he suggested that an American diplomatic presence in Urga—as Mongolia's capital city of Ulaanbaatar was then known—would prove "helpful" to Mongolia. In fact, the entire phrase used in the dispatch that Ferrin sent to his superiors at the State Department in Washington, D.C., in 1918 continues to resonate nearly a century later: if the United States were to open an office in Urga, he argued, it would almost certainly prove to be "*a most helpful factor in the development of a wonderful country.*"

Although Ferrin's plea was unsuccessful in his lifetime, this phrase—which recurs at several points in the narrative that follows—poignantly conveys in only a few words what many Americans, diplomats and ordinary citizens alike, aspire for out of the US-Mongolia relationship. From the view of many Americans who have visited, Mongolia is indeed a "wonderful country," one that includes a fascinating history, vibrant culture and inspiring landscapes. There is also a genuine desire on the part of many Americans to see Mongolia succeed in its efforts to emerge as an unqualified success story in Northeast Asia, one that shares important core values with the United States and can potentially set a positive example for others in the region and beyond.

History also resonates across important aspects of the relationship. For example, when Mongolia and the United States celebrated the 20th anniversary of bilateral relations in 2007, the Mongolian Postal Service issued a set of two stamps to mark the occasion. One stamp featured Genghis Khan cast in bronze, sitting on his throne in the large, recently completed memorial outside Government House in Sukhbaatar Square in downtown Ulaanbaatar. The other depicted President Abraham Lincoln cut from marble, also looking larger-than-life from the vantage point of the Lincoln Memorial on the Mall in Washington, D.C.

As shown on the stamps, the two huge sculptures are very similar, each showing a national hero seated in an almost identical pose that exudes power, confidence, and authority. Both stand out as leading historical figures and as instantly recognizable symbols of their respective countries. While different in many important respects, the juxtaposition of the two leaders in these commemorative stamps also serves to underscore that Genghis Khan had forged unity among the Mongol people during the thirteenth century, just as Abraham Lincoln six centuries later successfully fought to maintain the unity of the United States, helping to establish and sustain a "more perfect union." Although separated by different histories and cultures as well as thousands of miles and a huge ocean, perhaps it was inevitable that Mongolia and the United States—one an old nation that became a great power during the thirteenth century, the other a new country that emerged as a world power only in the twentieth century—would eventually meet.

There are, of course, several ways to analyze and critique relations between countries, including countries as different and as geographically far apart as Mongolia and the United States. One approach might be to highlight geopolitical issues, focusing on Mongolia's strategic location between two large powers, Russia to the north and China to the south. Another might be to focus on national interest, presenting US-Mongolia relations in either more pragmatic or more hard-headed terms as being primarily driven on both sides by the quest for national advantage, whether related to national security, the search for influence, or a concerted effort to gain commercial benefit. Certainly, the foreign relations of any country are based on a mix of ideology, idealism, and national interests.

All these issues and more inevitably arise when any two countries engage with each other seriously on the world stage. To complicate matters further, bilateral relations between countries are never conducted in a vacuum. On the contrary, they become increasingly pronounced when set against the reality of a wide and complex web of bilateral relationships involving other countries both near and far, as well as with a growing number of multilateral players. For Mongolia, forging an effective foreign policy that achieves an appropriate balance among many often competing priorities and potential partnerships will always remain as an especially formidable challenge that more or less defines and determines Mongolia's place in the world.

It is also the underlying rationale behind what is typically described as Mongolia's "third neighbor" approach to foreign policy. Since the early 1990s, every Mongolian government of all political persuasions has attempted to simultaneously maintain friendly ties with its "first" and "second" neighbors, Russia and China, while also reaching out to a wider world consisting of a multiplicity of "third neighbors," including Japan, Korea, India, Canada, Australia, the various countries forming the European Union, and the United States. Put another way, in recent years Mongolia has actively sought to maintain a "three-dimensional" foreign policy, one that consciously promotes positive and productive engagement with its two immediate neighbors while also seeking to build constructive ties with a much wider set of other countries, as well as a range of multilateral institutions situated in every corner of the world.

Against that backdrop, this book intentionally deals with only one set of "third neighbor" relationships—those involving the United States and Mongolia, two countries that have been interacting diplomatically for only a quarter century while maintaining a remarkable set of people-to-people ties for at least 150 years. The approach is primarily narrative and descriptive rather than highly critical or theoretical. It is not rooted in any grand theory of international relations or meant to become a platform for extended reflections on how nations compete, cooperate, or interact with each other within a wider geostrategic arena. Rather, it touches in significant part on the human dimensions of the US-Mongolian partnership as it has played out in a number of important areas over the last 25 years. More than anything, the intent here is to record and preserve some of the major highlights in an emerging and fascinating story, one in which many chapters remain to be written.

The narrative begins in the early 1860s, when the first American adventurers began arriving in "Outer Mongolia," a distant area on the map that at the time was seen as one of the most remote and forbidding places on earth. A subsequent chapter explores in greater depth the several "false starts" and "unexpected turns" that eventually culminated in the January 1987 agreement to establish relations, exchange ambassadors, open embassies, and engage in normal diplomatic relations.

Five successive chapters in turn assess and describe the several areas in which US-Mongolian ties have flourished over the last quarter century. In particular, these five chapters—which represent the "core" of this book—describe a multitude of efforts on the part of both Mongolians and Americans to support democracy, partner on development, build commercial ties, promote security, and sustain people-to-people relations.

A final chapter provides an overall assessment of the current state of the relationship while also taking a speculative look at possible future developments. Several annexes include, among other things, a listing of some of the major agreements signed between the two countries over the past 25 years. The texts of two official documents produced in the summer of 2011—one issued by the White House, the other by the United States Congress—highlight and summarize the major areas of cooperation and mutual support achieved during the first quarter century of what has become a vibrant diplomatic relationship.

The manuscript concludes with a section on major sources and further reading, providing details on books, articles, monographs, and other sources of information for those wishing to explore in greater depth some of the themes highlighted here. At the same time, it needs to be emphasized that many of the recollections on which this narrative is based are purely personal in nature and until now have never been written down anywhere.

Put another way, the catalyst for this effort was decidedly nonacademic in nature, reflecting instead a conscious and deliberate attempt to capture some of the early memories and anecdotes linked to the early diplomatic history of the United States and Mongolia before they disappear forever. This was aided by a willingness on the part of six of the first seven American ambassadors to Mongolia to contribute memories of their own. In addition, some of the first Mongolian staff to work at the US Embassy in Ulaanbaatar provided their recollections. Finally, as a participant in certain parts of that history—first as USAID country director in Mongolia from August 2001 until April 2004 and then as US ambassador to Mongolia from November 2009 until July 2012—my own perspective and personal views are inevitably reflected in certain passages in the text that follows.

My sincere hope is that this book will remind Americans and Mongolians alike of some of the more interesting and important aspects of their shared history during its critical early stages. Perhaps it will one day also provide useful raw material for further reflection, critique, and analysis on the part of others about an intriguing and increasingly complex diplomatic relationship that continues to unfold. Finally, it should be emphasized that the faults inherent in this approach are mine alone—and that the views expressed in this volume are those of the author and do not purport to reflect those of the US Department of State or the US government.

Chapter 1
Early Encounters

"I have found my country, the one I was born to know and love."

The accounts vary in content and the dates are not entirely clear, but in either 1899 or 1900 two young men briefly met at the central monastery in Urga, as Ulaanbaatar was then known. One was a prominent lama known as the eighth *Jebtsundambu*, who 11 years later would lead the Mongolian quest for freedom from the Qing Empire, emerging as the "Holy King" or "Bogd Khan" (1869–1924) of a newly independent state. The other was a young mining engineer from California named Herbert Hoover (1874–1965) who, 28 years later, would become the 31st president of the United States.

Hoover was working in China at the time. Part of his job involved taking long trips into the countryside by horseback, exploring for possible mineral wealth. In the first volume of his memoirs, published many years later under the title *Years of Adventure*, Hoover recalled: "One of these horseback journeys reached as far as Urga, the Mongol capital in the Gobi Desert. . . . The monotony of that trip was enlivened by a call on the Hutuktu Lama—a Living Buddha—through the introduction of a Swedish engineer who was building a telegraph line connecting Peking with Russia and the influence of his friend the Russian consul."

Hoover was still in his late 20s while the future Bogd Khan had only recently turned 30. According to Hoover's account, he arrived at Gandan Monastery to find the Living Buddha "riding a bicycle madly around the inner court." Few other details are available about the meeting that followed between the two future heads of state. However, Hoover does report that the young lama entertained his visitors "with a phonograph supplied with Russian records."

There are no records to indicate what the Mongolians thought of their brash and opinionated visitor. The brief meeting did, however, both reflect and foreshadow important aspects of the increasing number of encounters between Americans and Mongolians during those early years. For Americans, Mongolia represented an ancient civilization as well as an exotic destination, far removed from their day-to-day experience. For Mongolians, newly introduced inventions from Europe and North America such as bicycles, telegraph lines, and record players represented the wave of the future, precursors to new technology that during the coming years would become more widespread and eventually change the face of Mongolia forever.

****

Herbert Hoover was not the first American citizen to visit the capital of Mongolia. In the preceding decades, other adventurous compatriots crossed the Gobi Desert to see the area then labeled on maps as "Outer Mongolia." For some, the trip to Urga was part of a much longer journey, one that started in China and ended in Siberia.

The Mongolian National Archives contain evidence of these early visitors that includes an intriguing collection of ornate and colorful "travel passes" provided to various foreign visitors, allowing them to "transit" Mongolia. These documents date to the mid-nineteenth century, a time when first Europeans and then Americans began to travel the globe in growing numbers. One of these travel passes, written in Mongolian using a phonetic Manchu script, was given to a visitor explicitly identified as an "American." The travel pass is dated 1862, a time when Abraham Lincoln presided over a deeply divided United States that had only recently embarked on a protracted and bloody civil war that threatened its very existence. While the pass provided authorization to transit Mongolia, it also noted that no bribes should be solicited or collected at any point along the way. A facsimile copy of this 1862 travel pass is now part of the Tibetan and Mongolian collection at the Library of Congress in Washington, D.C., a gift from the Mongolian National Archives donated in January 2012 to help commemorate 25 years of US-Mongolia diplomatic relations.

The document also very possibly marks the launch of the first people-to-people ties involving nationals of both countries. According to the text, the

American visitor was named either "Mr. Felosi" or "Mr. Pelosi," and his traveling companion was from France. According to a subsequent report from the Mongolian border post at the Siberian border to supervisors back in Urga, the two travelers, accompanied by a Mongolian guide, were seen to arrive on camels and were at first thought to be from Russia.

A few years later, an American with a much more detailed surviving historical record—the journalist and travel writer Thomas W. Knox (1835–96)—traveled by horse and cart from Peking to Kyatka, following the old tea route that continued for another 3,000 miles to St. Petersburg. The author of 45 books, Knox wrote a 12-page account of his travels in an article entitled "A Journey through Mongolia" that was later published in the August 1868 issue of *Galaxy* magazine.

Born in New Hampshire, Knox gained his reputation as a controversial Civil War correspondent for the *New York Herald,* writing reports that angered both General Grant and General Sherman, two of the leading Union commanders of the war. His reporting from the Civil War was later published to considerable acclaim under the title *Camp-Fire and Cotton-Field.* Not long after the Civil War, Knox embarked on a round-the-world tour, including a memorable journey across China, Mongolia, and Russia that he later described in his best-selling book, *Overland through Asia.* Subsequently, he wrote about his travels in the Middle East in a volume entitled *Baksheesh.* Still later, he launched a highly successful series of adventure books for boys set in some of the most remote regions of the world.

According to Knox's Mongolia travelogue in *Galaxy* magazine, it was only in 1859 that the Chinese finally authorized foreigners to traverse the region on their way to Siberia, a trip that up until that point he describes as "about as feasible" as a journey to "the South Pole."

Knox's expressed admiration for the Mongolians he encountered during his travels, while also noting, "They are proud of tracing their ancestry to the soldiers that marched with Genghis Khan." He must have shared some of his experience in the American Civil War with his Mongolian traveling companions, noting at one point that "around their fires at night no stories are more eagerly heard than those of war, and he who can relate the most wonderful traditions of daring deeds may be certain of admiration and applause."

Knox's descriptions also provide fascinating glimpses of Mongolia as it used to be. At one point, he notes, "The country opens into a series of plains and gentle swells, not unlike the rolling prairies of Kansas and Nebraska." He observed trains of oxcarts along the way, some stretching for a mile or more. He also noted that "boiled mutton" was the "staple dish" of Mongolia, served "unaccompanied with capers or any other kind of sauce or seasoning," instead simply handed over "all dripping and steaming."

Fording the Tuul River just before entering Urga, Knox indicated that the camels had to be persuaded to cross "with clubs," having an "instinctive dread" of water, especially deep and flowing water. Recalling the eastern approaches to what is now Ulaanbaatar, he first described a small Chinese settlement (an old Taoist temple from that time still survives), followed by "large houses" occupied by Russians (near what is today the Orthodox Church and what was once the Russian Consulate). Finally reaching the city, he noted that it "is not laid out in streets like most Chinese towns; its by-ways and high-ways are narrow and crooked and form a network very puzzling to a stranger."

Looking back nearly 150 years later, Knox's few comments on the geopolitical situation in Mongolia seem highly prescient. For example, he characterized China's hold on Outer Mongolia as "not very strong," adding that the Mongolians seemed "indifferent to their rulers and ready at any decent provocation to throw off their yoke." He also suggested that Czarist Russia already had "an eye upon Mongolia" and was even then contemplating "taking it under the powerful protection of the double-headed eagle."

During subsequent decades, travel to Mongolia, while still an adventure, became more commonplace. Certainly, by the later part of the second half of the nineteenth century, a small but growing number of Americans from an increasingly wealthy United States began to find their way to Mongolia, whether as adventurers, missionaries, or merchants. These early contacts in turn eventually involved other American visitors, including both diplomats and tourists.

By the early 1900s, visitors from the United States were becoming much more frequent. Indeed, the name American *Denj*—an area of contemporary Ulaanbaatar just off Peace Avenue and near the Hotel Kempinski that was once known for the American businesses that congregated there—probably dates back at least 100 years. According to some accounts, these early American business executives imported Mongolia's very first car, a Model T Ford. Also, the first silent films ever seen in Mongolia were very possibly shown in the American *Denj*.

****

US diplomat and former ambassador to Russia, China, and the Ottoman Empire William Woodville Rockhill (1854–1914) was another early American traveler to Mongolia who left a written record behind. He passed through Urga at the conclusion of his ambassadorship to the Ottoman Empire and only a year before he died suddenly of a heart attack in Hawaii. Traveling with his wife via the Trans-Siberian railway in 1913, he took a weeklong detour to visit Outer Mongolia.

Among other things, Rockhill noted a strong desire on the part of Mongolians for "complete independence." He placed Mongolia's population at that time at 700,000—down considerably from the three million that his research suggested had lived in Mongolia during the mid-seventeenth century. Describing life in Mongolia's capital city just prior to the start of World War I, he commented that "trade prospered, order prevailed and the people were satisfied."

It is very likely that Rockhill was the first American diplomat to speak Tibetan as well as Mongolian, having visited both Tibet and Inner Mongolia in 1888–89 during a leave of absence from his assignment as a junior diplomat at the US legation in Peking. A scholar as well as a diplomat, he published a number of books and articles about his experiences, including *Land of the Lamas* and *Diary of a Journey through Tibet and Mongolia*. Rockhill donated his entire collection of 6,000 books on China, Tibet, and Mongolia to the Library of Congress in Washington, D.C., which is now the repository of one of the world's largest collections of written material related to Mongolia.

In a poignant footnote, the holdings of the Library of Congress also include a small diary maintained by a young diplomat—Thomas W. Haskins (1879–1908)—who accompanied Rockhill on at least one of his several trips to eastern China. The diary, presented to the Library of Congress as a gift in 2011 by relatives of Thomas Haskins, contains a brief description of a meeting involving Rockhill, Haskins, and the 13th Dalai Lama that took place in Wutaishan in June 1908. Less than a month later, Haskins—not yet 30 years old—passed away following a sudden illness, leaving a young widow to mourn his death.

Rockhill's own impressions of Mongolia during the early years of the twentieth century were not entirely positive. For example, he declared Urga a dirty city and was pessimistic about the country's economic prospects. That said, he also described Mongolians as "easy-going" and concluded that Mongolians had "good grounds" for striving for independence.

Rockhill's visit to Urga in 1913 was followed seven years later by that of another American diplomat, Charles Eberhardt (1871–1965). However, what distinguished Consul Eberhardt's five-day pioneering journey in 1920 is that he came under official State Department auspices, met with senior Mongolian officials, and returned with a strong recommendation to open what would have been the first official US diplomatic presence in Ulaanbaatar.

His recommendation reflected the fact that an increasing number of American citizens were living and working in Mongolia. Increasing American interest was evident as well, especially on the commercial front. For its part, Mongolia's early quest for independence included a concerted effort to reach out to other countries, among them the United States. Partly associated with the quest on the part of some Mongolians for "modernization," some Mongolians at the time even advocated the adoption of a Latin alphabet for their language.

* * * * * * *

Strangely enough, an American steamship built in New Jersey and launched in 1903 as the SS *Mongolia* also helped introduce the land of Genghis Khan into the American consciousness during the first decades of the twentieth century. Built for the Pacific Mail Steamship Company, the *Mongolia* for several years connected the western United States with Asia, bringing passengers in both directions, along with her sister ship, the SS *Manchuria*. A 13,000-ton vessel, the *Mongolia* was relatively large and accommodated more than 1,600 passengers, 350 of them in first-class luxury and 1,300 in steerage. During those years, the passenger lists from the *Mongolia* included intending Chinese emigrants who booked a one-way passage across the Pacific to California.

The *Mongolia*, by then already past her prime, was sold in August 1915 to the Atlantic Transport Line and quickly became a fixture on the sea route between New York and London. When Germany announced a submarine blockade around the United Kingdom, the *Mongolia* was armed with three six-inch deck guns as a form of self-defense. According to some accounts, it was the *Mongolia* that fired the first American shot when the United States entered World War I on the side of Britain and France, taking aim at a German U-boat in the North Atlantic and possibly sinking it. Another incident, widely reportedly across the United States at the time, was the death of two female nurses, Edith Ayers of Ohio and Helen Wood of Illinois, accidentally killed when a propellant cap exploded during a firing demonstration, sending shrapnel in every direction.

For most of the war, the SS *Mongolia*—now bearing the military appellation USS *Mongolia*—served as a troop ship, carrying thousands of American soldiers to Europe to join the fighting. After an armistice was signed in November 1918, the USS *Mongolia* continued its troop ship role, carrying thousands of battle-hardened veterans back to the United States to rejoin their families.

The *Mongolia*'s remaining career was much less memorable. For a time, she sailed between New York and Hamburg. Later, she was put on the route from New York to San Francisco, passing through the Panama Canal. In 1929, both the *Mongolia* and the *Manchuria* were bought by the Dollar Steamship Lines and renamed as the *President Fillmore* and *President Johnson*, an odd choice considering that Millard Fillmore and Andrew Johnson rank among the two least distinguished presidents in American history. In 1940 the *Mongolia* was sold and renamed again, this time as the *Panamanian*. Six years later, she ended her life as scrap in a wrecker's yard in Shanghai.

How did the *Mongolia* and her sister ship the *Manchuria* get their names? Almost certainly, they were named to reflect exotic and remote parts of the globe at the start of what became the "American Century," as part of a possibly unconscious attempt to begin to imprint the names of strange and distant places more firmly into the minds of the American imagination. There was logic, too, in selecting a specifically Asian place name, given the fact that the *Mongolia* was initially built to cross the Pacific and connect Asia with North America.

In retrospect, it is the role played by the *Mongolia* in ferrying Asian migrants across the Pacific to the western United States during the early 1900s that seems especially poignant. The fact that the *Mongolia* later engaged with a German U-boat, possibly fired the first American shots of World War I, featured in headlines across the United States following the accidental deaths of two war nurses, and was used to transport many thousands of young soldiers to the battlefront only adds to the interest. Mongolia may be a land-locked country—yet it also became the name for an American steamship from the "golden age" of steam travel, sailing for years across first the Pacific and then the Atlantic, regularly reminding tens of thousands of passengers over a period of many years about the distant land of Genghis Khan.

* * * * * * *

Of all the foreigners with ties to the United States to encounter Mongolia and write about it during the early part of the twentieth century, perhaps none is more fascinating or knew more about Mongolia than Frans August Larson (1870–1957), sometimes known as the "Duke of Mongolia." Born in poverty in rural Sweden, he was orphaned at the age of nine. Possibly viewing missionary service as a means of escape as well as a way to see the world, Larson joined a foreign mission society and was assigned to northern China in the late 1890s.

Larson learned Mongolian quickly and became adept at making friends, qualities that proved immensely important in 1900 when he led a group of 22 Swedish and American missionaries into the Gobi Desert, across Mongolia, and on to Siberia to escape the violence of the Boxer Rebellion then raging across many parts of China. The group that he rescued included his American wife and fellow missionary Mary Rogers and their two young children. Later, Larson became the first Christian and Missionary Alliance representative in Mongolia.

Larson's remarkable 1,000-mile journey across the Gobi Desert, through Mongolia, and on into Siberia in 1900 was only one milestone in a life of high adventure, one that saw him traverse the Gobi no less than 36 times on camel, horse, and even bicycle. He ultimately focused on business and politics more than missionary work, though his wife Mary continued working for the church throughout her life.

Larson's linguistic skills proved invaluable, and visiting diplomats typically sought his views on major issues of the day. Most notably, he helped organize the logistics for much better-known explorers such as the American Roy Chapman Andrews and the Swede Sven Hedin. He also knew many of the leading Mongolian personalities of the early 1900s, including the Bogd Khan and many of his ministers. Larson's first memoir—entitled *Duke of Mongolia*—reflects a deep admiration, respect, and affection for Mongolia. He describes himself as "fortunate" to have had the opportunity to "learn their language, their mode of living, their happiness, their sorrow and, so often, their sudden death."

Larson himself lived in both Inner and Outer Mongolia for nearly half a century, leaving only in 1939 when he was almost 70 years old and the threat of a second world war was already looming. Subsequently, he moved to the United States, where he lived through much of the 1940s and 1950s, first running a chicken farm in Alabama and then spending the remaining years of his remarkable life as a housing developer in California, interrupted only briefly by interludes in Sweden and Canada.

According to Larson's granddaughter Barbara Sitzman, memories of Mongolia figured prominently throughout Larson's retirement. "My childhood was sprinkled with real life adventure stories of wolves, Chinese bandits, *kumiss* (fermented mare's milk) and wild horse races," she recalled many years later. In her account, Larson's love of Mongolia was also reflected in two other activities that he enjoyed until the end of his long and eventful life: first, he routinely picked the winning horses at his local racetrack in California; and, second, he kept the family television tuned to wrestling shows.

* * * * * * *

Larson's knowledge of Mongolia proved enormously helpful to Roy Chapman Andrews (1884–1960), perhaps the most well-known American to interact with Mongolia in the decades prior to the establishment of formal diplomatic relations. "I have found my country," Andrews wrote after his first trip to Urga in 1918, "the one I was born to know and love." As for Urga, Andrews called it "the most fascinating city I have found in all my wanderings."

A larger-than-life figure, Roy Chapman Andrews, according to some accounts, was one of the inspirations for "Indiana Jones," the fictitious adventurer and explorer who launched an entire movie series. Andrews is best known today for his expeditions to the Gobi Desert during the 1920s, explorations that discovered new varieties of dinosaurs and demonstrated for the first time that dinosaurs hatched from eggs.

Born in Wisconsin, Andrews dreamed of a life of adventure from an early age. After attending Beloit College, he traveled to New York, where he worked as a janitor at the American Museum of Natural History because no other jobs were available. Sometime later, he managed to join the crew of two scientific expeditions, one focused on the Dutch East Indies (now Indonesia) and another involving exploration in the Arctic.

Several years later, Andrews began planning his first Gobi expedition, using Dodge cars to explore regions west of Beijing. Between 1922 and 1925, he mounted four expeditions to the Gobi and returned again for a final visit in 1930. "The Flaming Cliffs," one of the most evocative sites in the various expeditions that Andrews launched, is today on every tourist itinerary to Mongolia's South Gobi province, featuring bright red rock formations and stunning sunsets against the vast expanse of the Gobi that are as memorable and inspiring as when Andrews first observed them nearly a century ago. The books he wrote, such as *Across Mongolian Plains* and *The New Conquest of Central Asia*, continue to offer insights for those interested in the way that foreigners viewed Mongolia during the 1920s.

Andrews reached the height of his popularity in the United States during the 1920s and 1930s. A flamboyant and effective self-promoter, he became an especially well-known figure as a result of his contributions to *National Geographic* and his lecture tours. His accounts of his adventures in the Gobi Desert brought exotic sights and different perspectives into homes, schools, and libraries across depression-era America.

The perspective among Mongolian authorities at the time was much more mixed, fed partly by the suspicion with which all things American were viewed among Mongolians in leadership positions and, most especially, by their Soviet patrons. Some expressed concern that he was a "spy," and others that he was simply robbing Mongolia of important aspects of its archaeological heritage. Viewed decades later, his written comments on both Mongolia and China very much reflect the tenor of the times, including a tendency toward broad characterizations and sweeping judgments that strike most present-day readers as little more than racist stereotyping.

Yet the photographs taken on his various expeditions, as well as the written descriptions that he left behind, help document a part of Mongolia as it used to be, providing fleeting insights into a way of life that was on the verge of disappearing forever. More recently, contemporary Mongolians have been intrigued by the photographs, which resonate especially among those seeking to retrieve something of Mongolia's lost past. Indeed, as one of several events organized in 2012 to mark the 25th anniversary of US-Mongolia diplomatic relations, one Mongolian television station visited the American Museum of Natural History in New York and produced a documentary focused entirely on Andrews and his various expeditions. At least one of the several books written by Andrews about his experiences in Mongolia—*On the Trail of Ancient Man*—was in 2010 translated and published in Mongolian.

Although Roy Chapman Andrews ranks as the best known among those Americans who traveled to Mongolia during the 1920s, he is by no means the only one. For example, General Joseph Stillwell (1883–1946), later a four-star general famous for his role in both China and Burma during World War II, was one of an increasing number of Americans to travel to Urga to see the sights of what was then regarded as an exotic as well as exceptionally remote part of the world.

Similarly, the prolific travel writer Harry Franck (1881–1962) drove from Kalgan in China to Ude in Siberia in 1922, passing through Urga en route. He later chronicled his travels in a volume entitled *Wandering in Northern China*. At about the same time, Janet Elliott Wulsin (1894–1963) from New York was in the middle of a four-year series of journeys through China, Mongolia, and Tibet along with her husband Frederick, an anthropologist. An account of their travels was later published in *National Geographic* in 1926.

Born into a wealthy New York family, Janet Wulsin had served in France as a Red Cross nurse during World War I. She met her future husband Frederick Wulsin, a Harvard University graduate from Ohio, in Paris. Apparently inspired by the example of Roy Chapman Andrews, they mounted their own expedition to China, Tibet, and Outer Mongolia. The couple later divorced and it was only after Janet Wulsin's death that her daughter Mabel Cabot, discovering her mother's letters and diaries, published a fascinating book called *Vanished Kingdoms: A Woman Explorer in Tibet, China and Mongolia, 1921–1925*. The striking hand-colored photographs taken by Janet and Frederick Wulsin are maintained in the archives of Harvard University's Peabody Museum, providing a series of brilliant and highly informative early images from across the region.

* * * * * * *

By the late 1920s, Mongolia was firmly part of the Soviet orbit, and the brief yet intense series of early American encounters with Mongolia already appeared to be receding into history. However, even during this period there was at least one notable meeting, this time involving US vice president Henry Wallace (1888–1965).

Regarded as one of the outstanding progressive intellectuals of his day, Wallace displayed a keen interest in Eastern religions. For a time he fell under the spell of the Russian-American artist, writer, and mystic Nicholas Roerich (1874–1947), who had lived in a small log cabin in Ulaanbaatar during 1926–27. Remarkably, Roerich's log cabin still survives—located just off Peace Avenue east of Sukhbaatar Square, it was turned into a small museum in 2009. It also serves as one of the few remaining architectural examples from the time when the buildings of Ulaanbataar were mostly made of wood and built in a Russian style.

Wallace's early ties with Nicholas Roerich were later seen as a source of potential embarrassment, especially in 1948, when he ran for president. Decades earlier, Wallace had opened his awe-struck letters to Roerich with the remarkable phrase "Dear Guru," an indication of the respect he had held for Roerich at the time. Later, as secretary of agriculture, Wallace provided direct support to Roerich's controversial and ultimately unsuccessful expedition to China, Manchuria, and Mongolia in the 1930s to search for drought-resistant grasses.

Almost certainly, Wallace would have recalled these earlier connections with Mongolia when he briefly visited Ulaanbaatar in early July 1944 at the end of a long journey that also included China, Siberia, and Soviet Central Asia. On arrival at Ulaanbaatar Airport, he was met by Marshal Choibalsan and many thousands of ordinary and no doubt curious Mongolians who had never seen an American before. At the time, the entire population of Ulaanbaatar did not yet exceed 100,000, while the entire population of Mongolia was estimated at around 1.5 million.

During his brief visit to Mongolia, Wallace was entertained by a folk opera, slept in a *ger* (what the Russians call a yurt), was presented with a *deel* (traditional Mongolian clothing), and visited two herder families. He also attended several pre-*Naadam* events, in anticipation of Mongolia's annual cultural festival, and was shown some of the "classic" sites featured in most tours of Ulaanbaatar to this day, including the Bogd Khan's winter palace. He was also given a pair of riding boots as well as a bow and arrows—and a selection of Mongolian stamps to pass on to President Franklin Roosevelt, an avid stamp collector. While originally scheduled to stay in Ulaanbaatar for just one night, Wallace ended up having to stay for two, spending an extra day in Mongolia after his flight to Chita in Siberia was turned back because of bad weather.

Although not entirely supported by the historical record, some Mongolians credit Wallace's apparent interest in wanting to see Gandan Monastery as a useful gesture in restoring some measure of respect for Buddhism and perhaps even "saving" the landmark monastery at a time when hundreds of other monasteries had been destroyed and religion was being actively suppressed across the country. Even today, there are Mongolians who claim that Wallace's desire to see Gandan Monastery might have helped spare it from destruction, as was the fate of so many other Mongolian monasteries throughout the darker years of the Soviet period.

In reality, Wallace sometimes referred to Buddhism in Mongolia in less than flattering terms. For example, at one point in a travelogue published after his return to the United States under the title *Soviet Asia Mission*, he noted appreciatively that Mongolia had been "freed of the monkish control of pasture land." His comments on Mongolian lamas occasionally took on a negative tone, at one point referring to them as a "robust though shiftless lot."

Wallace was accompanied on his 1944 trip to Ulaanbaatar by Owen Lattimore (1900–89), an American scholar and foreign policy advisor who was regarded as one of the first great American specialists to study, research, and write on Mongolia. Born in the United States but partly raised in China, where his parents taught English at a local university, he worked variously as a journalist, editor, researcher, scholar, and businessman. Lattimore traveled extensively across East and Central Asia and spoke both Chinese and Mongolian. A prolific writer, he authored many books, including *The Desert Road to Turkestan, High Tartary, The Mongols of Manchuria, Mongol Journeys,* and *Nomads and Commissars: Mongolia Revisited.*

During the 1950s, Lattimore was accused of being overly sympathetic to the Soviet Union and Communist China. As a result, he faced a grueling attack in Congress led by Senator Joseph McCarthy. He subsequently moved to England and in 1963 became the first professor of Chinese studies at the University of

Leeds. While at Leeds, he maintained and even deepened his strong interest in Mongolia, which he visited regularly throughout the 1960s and 1970s. In 1967, Lattimore also became the first American—indeed, the first Westerner—to be elected to the Mongolian Academy of Science.

****

While the 1960s are typically viewed as a period in which there was virtually no contact between the United States and Mongolia, a handful of intrepid tourists and an even smaller number of prominent Americans continued to make their way to what Vice President Wallace had described during his own travels as "one of the most remote regions of the world." Perhaps most notably, the well-known *New York Times* journalist Harrison Salisbury (1908–93) visited Mongolia in 1959. He was followed not long afterwards by US Supreme Court Justice William O. Douglas (1898–1980) who subsequently wrote up his impressions of the Mongolian steppe in an article for *National Geographic* under the title "Journey to Outer Mongolia," published in 1962. Douglas also wrote an article for the *New York Times* making the case for US recognition of Mongolia as an independent state.

Several notable academics, some of them emigrants to the United States from other countries, kept the study of Mongolia alive in the United States during the Cold War period, despite the fact that the United States had not yet recognized Mongolia as an independent state. These include Nicholas Poppe (1897–1991) at the University of Washington; Francis Cleaves (1911–95) and Joseph Fletcher (1934–84) at Harvard University; Denis Sinor (1916–2011) and Gombojab Hangin (1921–89) at Indiana University; and Henry Schwarz (1928–) at Western Washington University.

In the absence of any official political or economic ties, it was the work, dedication, and commitment of these and other academics that maintained and even expanded interest and knowledge about Mongolia in a number of colleges and universities across the United States. Some schools—including Indiana, the University of California at Berkeley, Brigham Young, Columbia, Harvard, Johns Hopkins, and Western Washington—even offered Mongolian language courses on occasion. In addition, they supported Mongolian-related research, sometimes funded by the US Office of Education or the National Endowment for the Humanities.

Founded in 1961 and located at Indiana University, the Mongolia Society also represented an important early effort on the part of American academics and others to maintain interest, support research, and publish material on Mongolia, making it available to a larger English-speaking audience. Headed by Alicia Campi at the time, the Mongolia Society celebrated its 50th anniversary in 2011. Its various publications—including *Mongolian Survey* and *Mongolian Studies: Journal of the Mongolia Society*—remain important sources of information in English about Mongolia, both past and present.

Despite these and other efforts, Mongolia remained a strange and exotic place for most Americans throughout the Cold War period. More usually, when "Outer Mongolia" was mentioned at all during the 1950s and even well into the 1960s and 1970s, it was as a very distant place, as remote and far removed from the United States as it was possible to imagine.

Chapter 2
Establishing Diplomatic Relations

"If America had a consul at Urga . . . it would be a most helpful factor in the development of a wonderful country."

The establishment of formal diplomatic ties between Mongolia and the United States on January 27, 1987, introduced a new chapter in the US-Mongolian encounter, one that was given further impetus with Mongolia's "decision for democracy" during the tumultuous and historic events of 1990 and afterwards. Over the past quarter century, these diplomatic ties have also become the foundation and springboard for a growing network of relationships in at least five other main areas—democratic exchanges; development assistance; commercial opportunity; security cooperation; and people-to-people engagement.

Initial diplomatic contacts between the United States and Mongolia were first launched during the early 1900s. However, it would take many decades for formal diplomatic ties to be officially established. Political developments within the United States played a partial role in preventing this from happening. Additionally, there were times when efforts by the United States to open relations with Mongolia were not reciprocated on the Mongolian side, usually because of pressure from the Soviet Union. In retrospect, synchronizing diplomatic overtures between the two countries proved to be an unexpectedly difficult task.

Mongolia marks 1911 as the date of its official proclamation of independence. According to documents maintained in the Mongolian National Archives, by November 1912 the new government headed by the Bogd Khan sent letters to several countries, including France, Germany, Belgium, Japan, Denmark, the Netherlands, the Austro-Hungarian Empire, the United Kingdom, and the

United States. Among other things, the letters announced Mongolian independence to the leading nations of the world while also requesting "friendly cooperation."

Records from that time further suggest that in 1914 the Bogd Khan's government wrote to the United States legation in Peking, requesting that a consulate be opened in Urga, as Ulaanbaatar was then known. Four years later, A. W. Ferrin—the US trade envoy in China—recommended to Washington that the United States do exactly that, further suggesting in his memorable turn of phrase that "if America had a consul at Urga . . . it would be a most helpful factor in the development of a wonderful country."

In 1919, Commercial Attaché Julean Arnold made a similar recommendation. Highlighting economic opportunities in particular, Arnold placed Mongolia's annual exports at around $15 million and argued, "It is the psychological moment for the inauguration of American activity in Mongolia." When Washington finally replied on the question of a US consulate in Urga, it resorted to the classic language of bureaucratic obfuscation everywhere, rejecting any immediate steps while not necessarily closing the door permanently: "It is not deemed practicable to establish an office at the present time."

* * * * * * *

Although formal recognition of an independent Mongolia was still more than half a century away, during the early 1920s the United States did open a consulate in the Inner Mongolian city of Kalgan, known today in China as Zhangjiakou. The purpose was to track political developments in Outer Mongolia, promote trade, and protect the interests of the handful of American citizens then living in both Inner and Outer Mongolia.

Located 135 miles northwest of Beijing and 600 miles southeast of Urga, Kalgan was a trading center with a population of 30,000, including many ethnic Mongols. The completion of a rail line from Peking to Kalgan in October 1909 had given the city added importance. Several companies with American connections—including Standard Oil, the British-American Tobacco Company, and the Mongolian Trade Company—all had American staff working out of Kalgan who often visited Mongolia to advance their business interests. Enterprising American business executives also pioneered an early automobile route connecting Kalgan with Urga. At one point, as many as 15 American cars—a combination of rugged Fords and dependable Dodges—plied the Kalgan-Urga route, providing a useful taxi service for both goods and passengers across the Gobi Desert.

Samuel Sokobin (1893–1986) was the first US consular official assigned to Kalgan, serving initially as interim consul and then as consul. Occasionally, he also visited Urga, providing the State Department in Washington with a first-hand perspective on people and events in a rapidly changing Outer Mongolia, one that for a brief time was emerging as an unlikely "battleground" for both White Russians and Bolsheviks fighting for supremacy across the vastness of the Russian Empire.

During this period of violence and instability, Mongolia witnessed a number of dramatic events outside the scope of any discussion on US-Mongolian relations. Among the most notable were the final expulsion of the remaining Chinese troops garrisoned in Mongolia and the brief but devastating rule of a savage and enigmatic character known as the "Mad Baron," who for a time provided White Russians with the illusory hope that they might yet defeat the Bolsheviks.

The Mad Baron's full name was Roman Nikolai Maximilian von Ungern-Sternberg, and he was born to Baltic German parents in Austria in 1895. He later attended military school in St. Petersburg, served in a Cossack regiment in eastern Siberia, and first visited Mongolia when he was briefly assigned to help guard the Russian Consulate in the important city of Hovd in western Mongolia prior to the onset of World War I. Later, amidst the chaos of the Bolshevik Revolution, he simultaneously dreamed of restoring both the Romanov dynasty and the Mongol Empire. Increasingly viewed as unstable if not demented, the "Mad Baron" succeeded in expelling the Chinese from Urga, making the city his base during the early weeks of 1921. However, his ruthless reign was short-lived. In August 1921 he was captured by the Bolsheviks in north-central Mongolia; and in September 1921 he was tried and executed across the border in Siberia.

Yet, even in the uncertainty that marked so much of the early 1920s, there were opportunities for American commercial activity (as reflected in the entrepreneurship of the Swedish-American businessman and former missionary Frans Larson); scientific enquiry (as Roy Chapman Andrews demonstrated in his various expeditions to the Gobi); and tourism (as suggested by the travel writing of Harry Franck). For their part, Mongolians consciously reached out to the wider world, typically welcoming ties with foreigners of any type and especially those from Europe and North America, who were perceived to provide important "balance" at a time when Mongolia, while ending its ties with China, was increasingly falling within the Soviet orbit.

Lacking any formal presence in Mongolia, the United States largely watched events unfold from a distance. Officially, the doors of the new American Consulate in Kalgan, housed in a building leased from Frans Larson, first opened on April 1, 1921. As the first American consul in Kalgan, Sokobin sent periodic reports to his superiors in Peking that on occasion touched on both political developments and commercial opportunities in Outer Mongolia.

In addition, Sokobin's tenure at Kalgan as well as that of his two successors—Edwin Stanton and Lewis Clark—provided important opportunities for occasional contact with senior Mongolian officials, contact that was maintained even in the absence of formal diplomatic ties or an exchange of ambassadors. In August 1921, the same month in which the Bolsheviks finally captured the "Mad Baron," Sokobin drove across the Gobi Desert in his initial foray to Urga and got lost for two days before eventually finding his way to Mongolia's capital city. He stayed in Urga for a month, sufficient time to provide useful reporting on political and economic developments as early Mongolian nationalists sought to strengthen and develop diplomatic and trade relations with the rest of the world beyond Russia and China.

On various occasions, Sokobin met with Prime Minister Dogsomyn Bodoo and several Mongolian cabinet ministers, including modern Mongolia's "founding father," Sukhbaatar, then serving as minister of war. At times, Frans Larson accompanied him as a translator. According to contemporary accounts, Bodoo expressed hope that "the American government would be the first to recognize the new, independent state of Mongolia." Subsequently, Bodoo sent a note "proposing the establishment of friendly relations between the two countries, especially trade relations." The prime minister also requested a "treaty," "a resident ambassador," and "commercial relations," all meant to "increase benefits to both countries." In November 1921, in an article Bodoo wrote for *The Nation* entitled "Mongolia Speaks to the World," he expounded on similar themes, including the case for establishing friendly ties between the United States and Mongolia.

In the end, Bodoo's term as prime minister proved to be brief. Born in 1885, he spoke Mongolian, Tibetan, Manchu, and Chinese and had once served as a lama, an occupation the Soviets deemed reprehensible. Later he worked as a translator at the Russian consulate in Urga before embarking on a revolutionary path that eventually led him to help found the Mongolian People's Party and, in 1920, travel to the Soviet Union to discuss future plans for the country under Soviet guardianship. He served as prime minister of Mongolia from April 1921 until January 1922, when he asked to be relieved of his responsibilities, ostensibly for health reasons. Several months after that, he was arrested and then executed.

Sokobin visited Urga at least four times during his tenure as head of the American consulate in Kalgan during the early 1920s, developing a useful network of contacts, both Mongolian and foreign. However, the Soviets were highly suspicious of his efforts, and the hoped-for rapid expansion in commercial opportunities involving American companies never materialized.

The fate of Soliin Danzan, a key early player in the Mongolian Revolution who briefly served as minister of finance, illustrates the formidable hurdles that prevented even commercial ties from developing. At one point, Danzan had represented the American-Mongolian automobile company in Urga. Reportedly, he owned private houses and cars— and a Harley Davidson motorcycle given to him by the American businessman W. Holman. An early advocate of capitalism in the Mongolian context, he was executed in 1924 as the revolution turned once more on one of its early proponents and claimed yet another victim. As with Prime Minister Bodoo, the lesson was obvious enough: working with Americans or, for that matter, any other foreigners, might easily prove fatal.

The complete consolidation of the Soviet hold in Mongolia effectively ended any hope of expanded trade relations, at least for American business. On September 30, 1927, the small US consulate in Kalgan finally closed down, having been in place for little more than six years. With the closure of the consulate, the US "window" on Outer Mongolia was also shut tight, ushering in a period of long diplomatic silence in which the United States lacked not only an official presence in Mongolia but also the insights provided by even the occasional diplomatic visitor.

* * * * * * *

Few Americans visited Mongolia during most of the 1930s and for much of the early 1940s, a period that included almost complete disengagement by China combined with an ever-stronger Soviet presence. These were dark days for Mongolia, as Stalin exerted an increasingly harsh hand and the Soviet impact became more and more evident, even in remote areas of the countryside.

On the American side, there was little knowledge of what was happening domestically within Mongolia or about the pogroms launched by Stalin that decimated Mongolia's traditional Buddhist community, destroyed hundreds of monasteries, and resulted in the deaths of many thousands of Mongolian lamas, intellectuals, military officials, and party cadres, some of whom were accused of being "spies" for various foreign powers, most notably Japan.

Even the battle of Khalkin Gol, which took place in the summer of 1939 along Mongolia's eastern border with Manchuria, remained largely unnoticed in the United States, despite the potentially far-reaching and even historic implications that it set in motion. The battle pitted a combined Mongolian-Soviet force led by General (later Marshal) Zhukov against a large Japanese army seeking to expand Japan's own empire into Mongolia and perhaps Siberia. The battle itself began with an initial skirmish in May 1939 and lasted until August 1939, eventually involving airplanes and tanks as well as cavalry on horseback.

By some accounts, the overwhelming Japanese defeat at this desolate and remote site led Japan to reorient its strategic perspective away from Northeast Asia and toward Southeast Asia, in turn contributing to its decision to invade Burma, Malaya, Singapore, French Indochina, the Dutch East Indies, and the Philippines—and, ultimately, to protect its far eastern flank and keep the United States at bay, even contributing to Japan's decision to attack Pearl Harbor. Though such possibilities have been ignored in most history books for years, Antony Beevor's popular one-volume *Second World War*, published in 2012, does in fact recognize this connection. Beevor departs from the more usual opening references to Germany's invasion of Poland in August 1939 and instead starts his narrative by describing the devastating Japanese defeat at the hands of the Soviets and Mongolians at Khalkin Gol, using the battle as a platform to help shed light on the geopolitics of Europe as well as Asia.

More than 70 years later, the battle site at Kalkhin Gol on Mongolia's eastern border with China remains an isolated and rarely visited place, marked only by the occasional memorial or small cemetery stretching across the landscape. Even now, it is possible to explore the site and see the remnants of war, including rusting helmets, decaying hand grenades, corroding ration tins, crumbling shoes, and even the whitened bones of the fallen. The shallow remains of trenches and shell holes on the steppe are also visible, serving as reminders of the ferocity of the conflict. As one contemporary Mongolian marker—placed next to the remains of a bomb crater—poignantly notes, "Even now, the wounds of war have not completely healed."

While most of the more than 57,000 troops that Zhukov commanded at Khalkin Gol were Soviet, some 3,000 Mongolian soldiers also participated, drawing special praise for their horsemanship. Colonel (later General) Lkhagvasuren, aged 27 at the time, became the heroic face of battle for Mongolia, reminding Mongolians in subsequent generations of the honorable part that their ancestors played in the victory. During a trip to Arkhanghai in central Mongolia in February 2012 to celebrate *Tsagaan Sar* (the traditional Mongolian New Year), I met a 102-year-old veteran of Khalkin Gol being looked after by his family, blind but otherwise in good health, one of the few soldiers from that era who still survive. A statue of a youthful Lkhagvasuren, in uniform with a sword at his side, has also been erected in Ulaanbaatar, near the Selbe River at the end of Denver Street, a few hundred yards from where the US Embassy now stands.

* * * * * * *

World War II and the period that followed offered a potential new opportunity for the United States and Mongolia to engage on the diplomatic front. Remarkably, it was Mike Mansfield (1903–2001), then a young congressman and later a revered senior statesman, who was one of the first to raise the issue of US recognition.

Mansfield, though born in New York, was raised, educated, and taught for a decade in Montana, the US state said to most resemble Mongolia in terms of its small population and vast, impressive landscapes. Mansfield himself never visited Mongolia, but from a distance he became a firm champion of it. Years later, as US ambassador to Japan, he once again had an opportunity to promote his goal of recognizing Mongolia as an independent state and establishing diplomatic relations between Mongolia and the United States.

Mansfield publicly endorsed US recognition of Mongolia as an independent state in the Congress on at least two occasions, first in the early 1940s as a member of the House of Representatives and again, some two decades later, as a senator. On the latter occasion, he referred to Harrison Salisbury's reporting in the *New York Times* and emphasized that Mongolia was neither a province of the Soviet Union nor a part of China.

Mansfield's speech on the floor of the Senate in 1960 became a catalyst for subsequent discussion of recognition in the early days of the Kennedy administration. Pushback came from other politicians and some sections of the media, which expressed skepticism and argued against it. As a result, efforts to extend US recognition of Mongolia as an independent state once again foundered and petered out.

The United States did ultimately acquiesce to Mongolia's successful effort, under Soviet patronage, to join the United Nations in October 1961, abstaining on the matter rather than voting against it. Shortly thereafter, a German-born Jewish realtor named Walter Sheldon assisted Mongolia in obtaining property in which to house its Mission to the United Nations. Having worked as a businessman in Inner Mongolia during the 1920s, he was especially sensitive as well as sympathetic to Mongolian requirements and was ultimately successful in arranging not only the purchase of a building in New York City but also a summer property on Long Island.

For the early Mongolian diplomats assigned to the United Nations, life in New York provided a firsthand look at a country that for them had been mostly a mystery. Recalling a conversation with one of those early diplomats, Erdenechuluun, former US ambassador to Mongolia Al La Porta notes that many Mongolians had been "propagandized" into believing that the United States was an "armed camp" that was "dedicated to make war on the USSR."

As a USAID officer in Mongolia during the early 2000s, I recall meeting Mongolians whose parents had worked at the Mongolian Mission to the United Nations and who had spent part of their childhoods in New York, attending Russian schools and spending vacations on the Mongolian-owned summer facility on Long Island. According to their accounts, they lived physically in the United States but remained very much apart from it, mostly viewing New York and its surrounding areas as "outsiders." They remembered being intrigued by the United States as children, while remaining largely insulated from it.

Personal experience ultimately did result in changed perspectives on the part of at least some Mongolians, despite limited travel opportunities. For example, reciprocal travel restrictions similar to those imposed on the Soviet Union meant that Mongolian diplomats assigned to the United Nations were limited to New York City and their Long Island compound. Despite these restrictions, some Mongolian diplomats began to question the heavy-handed guidance from Moscow and to develop a different and more independent perspective on what the United States had to offer, both as an example and as a diplomatic player within the wider international community.

****

In January 1963, the United Kingdom became the first Western European country to officially recognize Mongolia and open an embassy in Ulaanbaatar. Anticipating that US recognition as well as the formal establishment of diplomatic relations might follow within the next few years, the Department of State at about the same time sent two young Foreign Service officers—Curtis Kamman (later US ambassador to Chile, Bolivia, and Colombia) and J. Stapleton Roy (later US ambassador to Singapore, China, and Indonesia)—to study Mongolian at the University of Washington in Seattle. Not long afterwards, Kamman traveled to Ulaanbaatar to participate in a United Nations meeting concerned with women's issues.

France was the next Western country to establish ties with Mongolia when it extended recognition and opened diplomatic relations in April 1965, followed thereafter by a concerted effort on the part of other Western countries to do likewise. However, despite occasional overtures from both Mongolia and the United States throughout the 1960s and into the 1970s, the time did not yet appear ripe to recognize Mongolia as an independent state, formalize a diplomatic relationship, and exchange ambassadors.

Partly, this was because the United States continued to maintain strong ties with the Nationalist Chinese in Taipei, which claimed Mongolia as part of their territory, in contrast to the Communist Chinese in Beijing, who had recognized Mongolian independence in 1946. As Richard Solomon, a former US assistant secretary of state for East Asia and the Pacific, recalled years later, President Kennedy in 1962 had "floated the idea of recognizing Mongolia." However, "Chiang Kai-shek shot the idea down because he considered Outer Mongolia as Chinese turf."

For their part, outreach by Mongolian authorities to the United States occasionally included pro forma contact with the American Communist Party. For example, a document in the Mongolian National Archives dated September 9, 1966, extends an invitation from the Mongolian People's Revolutionary Party (MPRP) to Gus Hall, head of the United States Communist Party, to visit Mongolia. Seven years later, in 1973, James Jackson, a member of the US Communist Party did in fact travel to Ulaanbaatar, where he met with Prime Minister Tsedenbal.

Media interest was also part of the mix. Among other things, this included interviews by United Press International (UPI) correspondent Albert Axelbank with Tsedenbal and Deputy Foreign Minister Dugersuren in spring 1968; an interview by *New York Times* correspondent C. L. Sulzberger in March 1971 with Prime Minister Tsedenbal; and an interview by *Time* reporter David Aikman with Foreign Minister Rinchin in October 1971. These media contacts, in particular, helped renew awareness about Mongolia among American officials while also giving the American public important, if brief, glimpses into Mongolia, which still seemed a distant place.

* * * * * * *

As the end of the Vietnam War approached, the opportunity for the United States and Mongolia to recognize Mongolia, establish diplomatic relations, and exchange ambassadors seemed to gain new momentum. Reflecting renewed optimism on the part of the United States, another two young Foreign Service officers—William A. Brown (later US ambassador to Thailand and Israel) and Alynn Nathanson—were sent to study Mongolian, this time with Owen Lattimore at Leeds University in England. As former senior US diplomat Walter L. Cutler later recalled, "We produced a Mongolian-speaking Foreign Service officer but with no place to go."

In spring 1973, American and Mongolian diplomats met several times in New York to discuss possibilities, hoping to prepare the groundwork for eventual recognition. However, just when it seemed that progress was being made, the Soviet Union made it clear that it would not approve such a step, causing yet another initiative to founder. Despite a concrete expression of interest on the part of Secretary of State Henry Kissinger to visit Mongolia and rumors that President Nixon himself was contemplating such a trip, the effort lost traction, leading to several more years of frustrating inaction.

US attempts during the Carter administration to renew the discussion on recognition and the establishment of diplomatic relations also appeared to make little or no headway, despite the fact that President Carter told then Foreign Minister Dugersuren pointblank at a dinner for the heads of Asian delegations in New York, "We are ready to establish full diplomatic relations with Mongolia." Just as the United States had been reluctant to establish relations during the 1950s and early 1960s for its own reasons, now it was Mongolia—with guidance from the Soviet Union—that seemed determined to slow things down and postpone the inevitable.

By the mid-1980s, nearly 100 countries had recognized Mongolian independence and established diplomatic relations—but the United States was still not listed among them. Nonetheless, American journalists such as Seymour Topping from the *New York Times* occasionally visited Mongolia, prompting further discussion as to why normal relations had not yet been established.

Lack of a US presence also did not stand in the way of visits by the occasional tourist or big-game hunter, not to mention scholars and even diplomats. For example, in September 1984 Donald Johnson—then first secretary at the US embassy in Beijing and several years later the third US ambassador to Mongolia—visited Ulaanbaatar, meeting with Mongolian academics and officials at the Foreign Ministry.

While American journalists occasionally made forays into Mongolia, a handful of American scholars found opportunities to conduct research and offer perspectives of their own. Robert Rupen, for one, first at Stanford and later at the University of North Carolina, produced two books, *Mongols of the Twentieth Century* and *The Mongolian People's Republic*. While condemned by communist authorities in Ulaanbaatar during the Soviet era, in retrospect both books represent a useful contribution to scholarship on Mongolia in English, a commendable achievement given the difficult circumstances in which the required research had to be carried out.

In October 1985, Robert Scalapino of Berkeley—one of his generation's most prominent American scholars on Asia—led a study trip to Mongolia along with other American academics. Meeting with Chairman Batmonkh in Ulaanbaatar, Scalapino took the opportunity to highlight the importance of formal diplomatic ties between the United States and Mongolia.

The rapid changes stemming from *glasnost* and *perestroika* in the Soviet Union provided a new opportunity for dialogue as well as new grounds for hope on the diplomatic front, despite the deep frustrations of the past. About this time US Foreign Service officer Curtis Kamman—by now head of the US interests section in Cuba—attended an exhibition sponsored by the Mongolian embassy in Havana. Apparently, some elements of the discussion that ensued were later reported back to Foreign Ministry authorities in Ulaanbaatar. At about the same time, discussions were also beginning to take place in Tokyo that would eventually help realize the long-standing goal of finalizing formal diplomatic ties between Mongolia and the United States.

Former Senator Mike Mansfield was by then US ambassador to Japan and a senior US statesman perceived in Ulaanbaatar as a sympathetic "friend" of Mongolia. Mansfield played a role in the unfolding diplomatic drama, which also involved Ravdan Bold, then a second secretary at the Mongolian embassy in Tokyo and later Mongolian ambassador to the United States.

Alicia Campi, at that time a young American diplomat who spoke some Mongolian and was working in the visa section of the US embassy in Tokyo, took a personal interest in the process, as viewed from her vantage point in Japan. Years later, she co-authored with R. Baasan a book about US-Mongolian relations during the twentieth century, published in 2009 under the title *The Impact of China and Russia on United States Mongolian Political Relations in the Twentieth Century*, that gave a detailed and indispensable account of the Mongolian quest for recognition, based on archival research conducted in both the United States and Mongolia.

According to Campi, starting in the fall of 1985 and continuing for at least a year, she and Bold occasionally met at downtown restaurants, coffee shops, and even Campi's own apartment on the US embassy compound in Tokyo. Reports from these meetings were shared with colleagues in Washington and with the US embassy in Beijing. For his part, Donald Johnson on his own initiative embarked on another long train trip from Beijing to Ulaanbaatar to explore the situation in Mongolia for a second time.

During his week at the Ulaanbaatar Hotel, conveniently located close to the Mongolian Foreign Ministry, Johnson eventually managed to meet with Davaagiiv, an English-speaking Mongolian official who later became his country's second ambassador to the United States. Yet the meeting was not successful, and subsequent reporting from the US embassy in Beijing to both Washington and Tokyo questioned the sincerity of Mongolia's commitment and its willingness to establish diplomatic ties with the United States anytime soon.

* * * * * * *

Despite these disappointments, the long journey toward recognition, launched decades earlier when the first American officials began to write about Mongolia, to visit Urga, and to recommend that the State Department recognize the independent state of Mongolia and establish a diplomatic presence there, was finally gaining an irreversible momentum. Following interaction between Campi and Bold in Tokyo and Johnson's two visits to Ulaanbaatar from Beijing, contact was established in New York between Ambassador Vernon Walters at the United States Mission to the UN and Ambassador Nyamdoo at the Mongolian Mission to the UN. Increasingly, there were also sympathetic go-ahead signals from President Gorbachev and Foreign Minister Shevardnadze in Moscow.

One important milestone was the meeting in New York on December 12, 1986, between Ambassador Nyamdoo and US Deputy Assistant Secretary of State for East Asia J. Stapleton Roy—the same Foreign Service officer who, almost a quarter century earlier, had spent a year studying Mongolian at the University of Washington in Seattle and had once thought he might eventually be posted in Ulaanbaatar. On this occasion, the US side passed on to the Mongolians a draft document outlining a framework for moving quickly on recognition and the establishment of diplomatic relations. A few days later, the Mongolian side returned the document with comments of their own.

Negotiations between the two sides continued into the early days of January 1987, and any lingering issues were quickly resolved. By mutual agreement, a date was also selected to mark the declaration of US recognition of Mongolia and the formal establishment of diplomatic relations between Mongolia and the United States: January 27, 1987.

Depending on the source, the United States became either the 100th or 101st country to recognize Mongolia. Secretary of State George P. Shultz made the official announcement for the United States. He also signed the relevant documents for the American side, even as Ambassador Nyamdoo signed for Mongolia.

Diplomats from both countries attended the small State Department ceremony held in the Treaty Room in Washington D.C., along with two private citizens who had worked so hard to promote relations over the years—John Gombojab Hangin, president of the Mongolian Society, who had emigrated to the United States from Inner Mongolia during the late 1940s; and Walter Sheldon, the far-sighted realtor who had helped Mongolia to locate property for its initial diplomatic presence in New York as a member of the United Nations more than 25 years earlier.

By coincidence, Joseph Lake—later the first US resident ambassador in Ulaanbaatar—was one of a small number of Foreign Service officers who attended the brief State Department ceremony. "I went to the secretary's office to work in the Operations Center in January 1987," he later recalled, and noted:

> Immediately after I arrived, the Mongolian ambassador to the UN and Secretary Shultz signed the agreement establishing diplomatic relations between the United States and Mongolia. I went out of historical curiosity as much as anything else, little realizing how relevant this would be in terms of my own personal future.

According to Lake, the next big challenge involved figuring out how to fund a new embassy in Ulaanbaatar at a time of severe budget constraints that were threatening the closure of consular posts in other countries. "The decision was made to fund it out of the hide of the existing East Asia Bureau on a real shoestring," he says, and adds: "I believe that 90 percent of the people who worked on it thought that this was a fundamental mistake."

Former US Ambassador to Mongolia Al La Porta—at the time serving in the Office of Management Planning with Under Secretary Ronald Spiers—amplified further on some of the bureaucratic in-fighting that made it difficult to contemplate opening a new embassy at a time when the State Department was dealing with its latest budget crisis. According to his account, it was Secretary of State Shultz who played an important role in "making the decision to cut through the bureaucratic and political fog on both sides." In La Porta's view, even at this late date there was opposition from some quarters, largely of a bureaucratic and administrative nature, that still required intervention by the secretary of state to overcome.

Back in Tokyo, Campi reports, when she and Bold heard that diplomatic relations had finally been established between the United States and Mongolia, they celebrated over "a steak dinner with champagne and cognac to toast the happy occasion."

****

Ambassador Nyamdoo moved from New York to Washington soon after, becoming Mongolia's first ambassador to the United States. Initially working out of an apartment building, Mongolia eventually turned a conveniently located former bank building on M Street in Georgetown into its embassy, a highly visible site where it remains to this day. The Mongolian Ministry of Foreign Affairs also bought an impressive residence for its ambassador in Potomac, Maryland.

Despite budget constraints that eventually resulted in the closure of several US consulates elsewhere, the US State Department moved forward with plans to establish an embassy in Ulaanbaatar. As Stapleton Roy noted in a conversation with a *New York Times* reporter at the time, Mongolia had "always been a place of fascination for Americans."

In early February 1987—only days after the signing ceremony in Washington—Stephen Young, a junior officer designated as one of the "Asia watchers" at the American embassy in Moscow (and later US ambassador to Kyrgyzstan, director of the American Institute in Taiwan, and consul general in Hong Kong) was dispatched to explore the situation on the ground in Ulaanbaatar, accompanied by Tom Hanson, a fellow Foreign Service officer. The two of them held meetings at the British, Japanese, Chinese, and Soviet embassies. Perhaps not surprisingly, their final report highlighted some of the enormous challenges involved in opening a year-round embassy in "the world's coldest capital" and expressed some skepticism as to whether the idea would even work.

In March 1987, Richard Williams, director of the State Department's Office of Chinese and Mongolian Affairs, made the first visit by a senior US official to Mongolia following the establishment of diplomatic relations, meeting with

Foreign Ministry officials and others in Ulaanbaatar. That summer a second US Foreign Service officer carried out further discussions, staying for several weeks at the Ulaanbaatar Hotel, the only housing then available. As Williams recalls:

> Our first concern following 1987 diplomatic recognition was basic—where would we work and live? Housing was so tight in the Ulaanbaatar of that era that for a long time there was no clear answer. At last, in the spring of 1988, we were able to open our first embassy when the authorities found us four 400-square-foot apartments in a building ordinarily reserved for other embassy drivers and cooks.
>
> We assigned two young Foreign Service officers, Steve Mann (later US ambassador to Turkmenistan) and Victoria Nuland (later US ambassador to NATO), to go out for the late spring and summer. They stayed in the upstairs flat, and the embassy office took up one of the two downstairs. That left the fourth little apartment as 'The Residence'—not only of the ambassador but of anybody else who managed to visit. Its unique endearing feature, unmatched elsewhere in the world, was the cow in the grassy yard outside who regularly wandered up to the window to stare in, chewing its cud in bovine amazement at the weird-looking foreigners.

On April 17, 1988, Steve Mann and Victoria Nuland transmitted cable Ulaanbaatar Number One, announcing, "Embassy Ulaanbaatar is open." Sent via Beijing at exactly 0503 hours "Zulu time," the cable reads as follows:

> 1. Arrived Ulaanbaatar 1050L April 17, assumed charge. Embassy Ulaanbaatar is open.
> 2. Until leased quarters are ready, Political-Economic-Officer Victoria Nuland and I will operate from the Hotel Ulaanbatar.
> 3. Cable traffic for Ulaanbaatar should be routed to Embassy Beijing. Unclassified traffic of priority precedence or higher will be relayed to Ulaanbaatar via telex from Beijing.

In fact, in the early days telex served as the main communications "lifeline" for the United States embassy in Ulaanbaatar. In one especially amusing early incident, the "Embassy of the US" was briefly confused with the "Embassy of the USSR," resulting in the following telex to Washington:

> At approximately 11:00 AM . . . we rcvd a phone call at this office from the USSR Embassy in UB saying that they had rcvd a commercial cable delivered to them by the Post Office which they suspected was for us. On pickup from the USSR Embassy we discovered it was addressed to "US Embassy

Ulaanbaatar" but apparently the Post Office made no distinction between "US" and "USSR" when sorting for delivery.

* * * * * * *

Following Senate confirmation hearings and a July presidential appointment as the first nonresident American ambassador to Mongolia, Richard Williams presented his credentials to Chairman Batmonkh in September 1988.

Some days later, Williams hosted a visit by US ambassador to the United Nations Vernon Walters, who had worked with Mongolian diplomats in New York to help prepare the groundwork for recognition and the establishment of diplomatic relations. Shortly thereafter, Williams, Mann, and Nuland all returned to Washington. Not until 1989, when more commodious housing became available, was the embassy finally staffed year-round.

In June 1989, Chargé Michael Senko and Theodore Nist arrived in Ulaanbaatar with their families, marking the start of regular two-year assignments in Mongolia for US Foreign Service officers volunteering to serve in what seemed like a cold, remote, and isolated part of the world. They were briefly joined by another Foreign Service officer—Alicia Campi, previously posted in Tokyo—who arrived to study Mongolian, undertake various public affairs assignments, and explore initial possibilities for what eventually became a long-term Peace Corps presence in Mongolia.

Photograph albums that are still maintained at the US embassy in Ulaanbaatar record a number of landmark early events, including the presentation of credentials by Ambassador Richard Williams and the unveiling of the first embassy plaque, both of which occurred in 1988.

At about the same time that Senko and Nist arrived in the summer of 1989, Luvsanjav was hired as the first US embassy employee from Mongolia. Another early Mongolian employee, Duinkerjav, with prior experience at the Mongolian UN Mission in New York, also made important contributions during those early years, when logistic and administrative challenges were especially formidable.

Embassy officials celebrated the Fourth of July with due fervor in Ulaanbaatar in 1989. Among other things, the festivities featured a round of fermented mare's milk known as *airag*, shared by Mike Senko with senior local officials, including Secretary of the Presidium of the Great People's Hural Gotov, Deputy Chairman of the Council of Ministers Peljee, and Foreign Minister Gombosuren.

The pioneering early embassy officers and their families arranged field trips and participated in a variety of local events, including the Mongolian Tennis Open held in September. A fading photograph from November 1989 shows the entire American staff and their families gathered around a Thanksgiving table—Chargé Mike Senko with his wife Dita and their children Sharon and Fe, aged 2 and 16 at the time, and Ted Nist and his wife Sally. Remarkably, Shannon, the Nist family dog, was subsequently used as a model by the Mongolian Post Office, her face forever preserved on a Mongolian postage stamp. The Senkos and the Nists were also the first American embassy families brave enough to spend an entire winter in Ulaanbaatar.

The following summer saw other landmark events, including the arrival of Joseph Lake as the first resident ambassador, followed almost immediately by a short visit by Secretary of State James A. Baker in early August 1990. Ambassador Lake traveled with his wife by train from Beijing to Ulaanbaatar to take up his new post, along with a group of Chinese workers headed to Romania and a shipment of watermelons rolling around the floor of the train compartment. Two weeks later, Secretary Baker arrived at Ulaanbaatar International Airport aboard Air Force Two. Although cows still grazed in front of the US Embassy, a newly paved road, informally dubbed "Baker Street," had also been built, just before the secretary's arrival.

In those early days, the US embassy offices in Ulaanbaatar were located in two places—first, in rooms 206 and 207 of the Ulaanbaatar Hotel, the same place where many other embassies, including the British and French, had initially established their offices on arrival some two decades earlier; and, second, in an apartment in a foreign residential complex controlled by the Mongolian Foreign Ministry. Ambassador Lake's first office was equipped with a discarded desk and table that had been turned over to the United States by the Japanese embassy. Space was at such a premium that the photocopy machine was placed on a board sitting atop a bathtub. Finally, in spring 1991, the American embassy moved to new and much larger quarters near the Selbe River, which remains the embassy location to this day.

Secretary Baker and his wife Susan visited Mongolia a second time in late July 1991. On this occasion, he accompanied Foreign Minister Gombosuren on a trip to the Gobi to see camels, eat mutton, and admire the desert landscape.

Returning to Ulaanbaatar, Secretary Baker joined Ambassador Lake in officially opening the newly refurbished US Embassy on the Selbe River. Photographs from the period also show him greeting the first group of Peace Corps volunteers in Mongolia and meeting with Chuck Howell, the first Peace Corps country director in Mongolia.

During the intervening years, the present Embassy complex has been improved and expanded. The building is leased from the Mongolian Foreign Ministry and, according to some reports, was initially designed to house the French and German embassies together, an interesting experiment in European harmony that never came to fruition. Regardless of its origin, the complex has been fully Americanized over the last two decades. It also continues to expand, marked most recently by the launch in summer 2011 of a new $25 million renovation program, providing suitable embassy facilities for at least the next generation.

Housing for American embassy staff has also improved markedly, despite many challenges. "We were prepared for spartan living," recalled Ambassador Al La Porta, who served in Ulaanbaatar during the late 1990s. "Our American staff in the beginning lived in a ramshackle ten-story apartment building called 'Faulty Towers,' located about 300 yards from the main Chancery building." Ambassador La Porta also recalled that Ulaanbaatar's first French restaurant, run by two Corsicans, opened soon after his arrival in Mongolia in 1997. At the time, the few restaurants in Ulaanbaatar were mostly located in Soviet-style hotels, providing poor food and appalling service.

It was only in 2001 under Ambassador John Dinger that embassy staff finally moved from Faulty Towers to the Star townhouse complex, built according to Czech standards near the railway line, on the road toward Zaisan and not far from Sukhbaatar Square. By spring 2004, some 17 career Americans were working at the US embassy in Ulaanbaatar. The size of the US embassy staff in Ulaanbaatar increased still further in subsequent years. By early 2012, a quarter century after that tiny first group of pioneering American diplomats arrived to locate apartments, there were more than 40 American officers working at the US embassy in Ulaanbaatar, assisted and supported by more than 160 Mongolian staff.

Chapter 3
Supporting Democracy

"It was an exciting moment to be in Mongolia as the country rediscovered its history and strived to build a democratic and free market future."

The establishment of diplomatic ties between the United States and Mongolia in January 1987 occurred on the eve of great international change, especially in the Soviet Union when Gorbachev's introduction of *glasnost* and *perestroika* gained traction and ushered in an era of transformation within the various former Soviet republics and beyond.

As a close neighbor of the Soviet Union, Mongolia was also drawn into this period of dramatic change. Many Mongolian students received their higher education either in the Soviet Union or in various Central European countries, including East Germany, Czechoslovakia, Poland, and Hungary. Some returned to Mongolia with new ideas as to how their country too might change course and move in a different direction. The prominent Mongolian writer and political commentator Baabar, for example, recalls his early contacts with the Solidarity movement while a student in Poland during the early 1970s—and the fact that he was jailed for translating Solzhenitsyn into Mongolian during the 1980s.

When the Berlin Wall was finally torn down in November 1989, the impact reached at least as far east as Ulaanbaatar. Indeed, some of the scenes during subsequent months on Ulaanbaatar's Sukhbaatar Square and elsewhere were reminiscent of similar events taking place in Central and Eastern Europe. As with many other allies of the former Soviet Union, Mongolia was part of a broad movement toward major change that favored both democracy and market-based economic reform.

The fact that the United States had recently established an embassy in Ulaanbaatar provided an important opportunity to observe the unfolding events at first hand. In early December 1989, proponents of Mongolia's emerging democracy movement celebrated Human Rights Day at the House of Youth in downtown Ulaanbaatar, initially drawing a crowd of around 200. The demands put forward by these peaceful demonstrators resonated with many other Mongolians, and the number of demonstrators quickly swelled to reach many thousands.

In March 1990, Chairman Batmonkh made the dramatic announcement that the entire Politburo would step down and a new government would be appointed. Gombojav Ochirbat then became the new chairman of the ruling Mongolian Revolutionary People's Party (MPRP). In May, First Deputy Prime Minister D. Byambasuren visited Washington. Mongolia, once one of the most isolated of countries, was finally beginning to open up to the wider world.

Not long afterwards—on May 4, 1990—Deputy Assistant Secretary of State Desaix Anderson, addressing the House Foreign Affairs Committee, affirmed that the United States had been "presented with unique opportunities to be supportive of positive developments at a turning point in Mongolia's history and at a time when their leaders are looking to us for assistance."

A few months later, Ambassador Joseph Lake, the first resident United States ambassador in Ulaanbaatar, attended the inauguration of Ochirbat, Mongolia's first democratically elected president. "It was a fascinating blend of Mongolian traditional culture and modern trappings," Lake observed:

> Ochirbat appeared for his inauguration wearing the traditional Mongolian *deel* and the traditional hat. The state seal was presented in a very traditional style, in a formal wooden box. The whole inaugural process was something that reached back to the roots of Mongolian history. One of the other currents developing in Mongolia at this time was the rediscovery of its own history.

* * * * * * *

Along with other democratic nations, in Europe and elsewhere, the United States reached out to Mongolia during the early 1990s to help support the country's efforts to move in a more democratic direction. Remembering those "heady" days, Lake recalled, "We received numerous requests for education and information" as Mongolia began to re-engage with other parts of the world. In fact, at one point the embassy even received an urgent phone call from an opposition member of parliament asking for a copy of *Robert's Rules of Order*.

"It was an exciting moment to be in Mongolia as the country rediscovered its history and strived to build a democratic and free market future," Ambassador Lake noted. "Even the simplest things which Americans saw as natural were new to Mongolians." According to Lake, the early American diplomats were received "with open arms." Moreover, "as change began to take place in Mongolia, the United States was idealized far beyond our capabilities and reality."

The Asia Foundation, based in San Francisco, was one of the first private US institutions to respond as Mongolia made its choice for democracy. It launched its first programs in 1990 and opened its resident office in Ulaanbaatar in 1991 when Shel Severinghaus arrived as the first resident country director. Even during the late 1980s, the Asia Foundation was approached by Mongolian government officials as the country began to reach out to broaden its engagement with the international community, both public and private. At the time, the very idea of a nongovernmental organization (NGO) was a new, strange, and even dangerous concept for most government officials in Mongolia.

During the early years, the Asia Foundation office in Mongolia established its presence in a rented log cabin in central Ulaanbaatar, reportedly one of the oldest permanent structures in the city. According to some accounts, the log cabin had once served as the residence of Sukhbaatar, the Mongolian revolutionary and nationalist hero.

This small log cabin, replete with history, soon became a useful meeting ground and a source of support and inspiration for Mongolia's rapidly emerging civil society, including a growing network of indigenous NGOs. Over time, the series of seminars, workshops, book distributions, and other outreach programs sponsored by the Asia Foundation proved instrumental in bringing international experience to bear as Mongolia faced new circumstances and worked through new challenges.

"The Asia Foundation was the pioneer that first worked with Mongolia's fledgling civil society, providing critical support and exchange opportunities to civil society leaders," recalls Chris Finch, the first executive director of the Mongolian Foundation for Open Society, the Soros-supported institution that later became known as the Open Society Forum. According to Finch, the Open Society Forum built on and in some cases expanded on the early Asia Foundation work.

Since 1991, the Asia Foundation has worked closely with Mongolian counterparts on a broad range of issues, many of them directly related to the establishment and support of democracy and civil society in Mongolia. Funding came from both private sources and the US government, including USAID and the Department of State. More recent programs include a focus on anticorruption, antitrafficking, and environmental concerns. In addition, the Asia Foundation has helped promote a national dialogue on Mongolia's rapidly growing mining sector.

Other American institutions contributed toward building democracy in Mongolia in various ways. US-based "political foundations" supported by private donations as well as the US government, such as the International Republican Institute (IRI), for example, have sponsored a wide range of democracy-related activities in Mongolia, helping to introduce Mongolian political leaders to American notions of how political parties forge coalitions, draft position papers, gauge popular opinion, and mount election campaigns. The National Democratic Institute (NDI) and National Endowment for Democracy (NED) share similar interests and have been similarly involved, though on a smaller scale.

IRI initiated its first program in Mongolia in 1991, sending speakers and technical experts to Mongolia. A couple of years later, it opened an in-country office in Ulaanbaatar, marking the start of a long-term, on-the-ground presence that provided firsthand experience in post-Soviet Mongolian politics, based on its ongoing work in the former Soviet Union and beyond. From the beginning, IRI committed itself to a nonpartisan approach, making its advice and training available to any political party that requested it.

Over the years, the IRI program in Mongolia concentrated on political party development, electoral systems, and capacity-building within Mongolia's parliament, the Great Hural. Famously, it introduced Mongolia's Democratic Party (DP) to the idea of a "Contract with Mongolia," along the lines of Newt Gingrich's "Contract with America," which had become part of the political discussion in the United States during the 1990s. Some commentators from both inside and outside Mongolia claim that it was the DP's use of this idea that helped catapult it to an unexpected victory in the 1996 parliamentary elections. While IRI was later criticized in some quarters for introducing American-style approaches to election politics in Mongolia, others welcomed the opportunity to learn from the American experience and adapt certain aspects of it to a Mongolian context.

Later, polling, focus groups, and public opinion analysis figured prominently in IRI's outreach and capacity-building efforts in Mongolia, based partly on the assumption that political parties need to shape their programs and policies in ways that respond to the views and positions espoused by an informed electorate. Twenty years later, IRI is still actively involved in Mongolia, albeit on a much smaller scale. More recently, the IRI programs in Mongolia have focused on decentralized development and grassroots democracy.

* * * * * *

"Hands-on" encounters in support of democracy include direct contact between American members of Congress and their Mongolian colleagues. Many Mongolian parliamentarians have visited Washington and discussed ideas with members of both the United States Senate and the House of Representatives, as members of the American Congress undertake similar dialogue in Ulaanbaatar.

According to Ambassador Lake, Senator Alan Cranston of California became the first sitting US member of Congress to visit Mongolia when he passed through Ulaanbaatar in August 1988. "Subsequently we had a visit by one member of Congress connected with IRI and then our first full-fledged Congressional Delegation (CODEL) in 1993."

Several members of the US House of Representatives have demonstrated a sustained interest in Mongolia over time, including Jim McDermott of Washington state, whose daughter taught math at the International School of Ulaanbaatar for several years. Representative Joe Pitts of Pennsylvania, who donated a fire truck and other equipment to Ulaanbaatar, was awarded Mongolia's "Polar Star" and has provided additional support to Mongolia in his role as chairman of the House US-Mongolia Friendship Caucus. In addition, current and former House speakers and minority leaders have visited Mongolia on a number of occasions.

During the late 2000s, the House Democracy Partnership (HDP) emerged as an important vehicle for promoting US-Mongolian parliamentary exchanges. A direct successor to the Frost-Solomon Task Force that assisted parliaments in Central and Eastern Europe during the early 1990s, the HDP was created in

2005. Two years later, the first programs in Mongolia were initiated. Fourteen other legislatures belong to the HDP partnership worldwide, including those in Kosovo, Afghanistan, East Timor, Georgia, and Peru.

As part of its core program, the HDP has co-ordinated several exchanges involving elected members and staff personnel, such as Representative David Price of North Carolina, who visited Mongolia in June 2011. Representative David Dreier of California visited on a regular basis over several years, including in August 2005, July 2007, and June 2011. Staff exchanges have been even more extensive and sometimes extend to third countries. For example, in 2009 a staffer from each of the Great Hural's seven standing committees participated in an HDP-sponsored training program in Macedonia.

Bipartisan Senate support helps further affirm congressional support for Mongolia's "decision for democracy." In October 2007, the Senate passed a resolution recognizing the 20th anniversary of diplomatic ties between the United States and Mongolia. Among other things, that resolution highlighted shared democratic values and expressed appreciation for the presence of Mongolian peacekeepers in Iraq, Afghanistan, Sierra Leone, and Kosovo. Resolution sponsors included Senator Lisa Murkowski of Alaska, Senator Richard Lugar of Indiana, and Senator Joseph Biden of Delaware. As vice president, Biden subsequently visited Mongolia in August 2011 during a trip through Northeast Asia that also included Japan and China.

Similarly, in June 2009—on the day of President Elbegdorj's inauguration—the US Senate passed another resolution, commending Mongolia for its democratic election and peaceful transition while also citing positive trends in its relationship with the United States. In addition to Senators Lugar and Murkowski, sponsors of this resolution included Senator John Kerry of Massachusetts and Senator James Webb of Virginia. A similar resolution was adopted in June 2011 in connection with President Elbegdorj's visit to Washington to meet with President Obama in the Oval Office, providing yet another opportunity to demonstrate official US support for Mongolia's continued commitment to democracy.

* * * * * * *

Undoubtedly, the signature event and most widely publicized expression of US support for Mongolia so far came on November 21, 2005, when President George W. Bush made his historic journey to Ulaanbaatar on Air Force One, accompanied by First Lady Laura Bush and Secretary of State Condoleezza Rice. As with many visitors, his itinerary included a visit to a *ger* along with a drink of *airag* and a cultural show featuring throat singing and Mongolia's traditional stringed instrument, the *morin huur*. He also addressed an audience of some 800 people at the State House and met with President Enkhbayar and then Prime Minister Elbegdorj.

On departing Mongolia, Bush declared, "I feel very much at home in your country." He also echoed comments shared by virtually every other American visitor to the high steppes of Mongolia, praising it as a "beautiful land, with huge skies and vast horizons." Subsequently, Mongolian postal authorities issued a commemorative stamp to honor and remember President Bush's historic visit. Beyond the platitudes and seemingly trite sentiments, President Bush's remarks reflected a genuine amazement, respect, and appreciation for Mongolia, a relatively small country that seemed to have chosen an unlikely and less well-traveled path, one very different from the one most of its neighbors had embarked upon during the post-Soviet era.

Vice President Biden's visit to Mongolia on August 22, 2011, garnered almost as many headlines as that of President Bush nearly six years earlier. Accompanied by his granddaughter Naomi, he arrived in Ulaanbaatar en route from China to Japan—the first US vice president to visit Mongolia since Henry Wallace's trip in July 1944, more than 67 years earlier. Vice President Biden's brief but packed schedule involved meetings at Government House with both President Elbegdorj and Prime Minister Batbold, among other events.

In his meetings at Government House, the vice president evoked well-worn themes emphasized by many senior visitors over the years, describing Mongolia as a "shining example for other nations in transition" and an "emerging leader in the worldwide democratic movement, a responsible actor on the world stage, and a close friend and partner of the United States." He also highlighted cooperation in other areas, including international peacekeeping and growing commercial ties. Concluding his official remarks, he stated, "We look forward to even closer ties in the years to come."

Privately, the American vice president urged the Mongolian government to strengthen the country's economic links with the United States while also going forward on a long-delayed "transparency agreement" aimed at improving Mongolia's business and commercial environment and making it more transparent. Contrary to what was reported in both the Mongolian and international press at the time, the issue of nuclear waste storage in Mongolia figured nowhere on the agenda and was not discussed at all.

Before departing from Mongolia after his brief visit, Vice President Biden and his party participated in a colorful encounter with Mongolian culture and traditions at Yarmag Denj, near Genghis Khan Airport, not far from where a similar event had been organized for Vice President Wallace nearly seven decades earlier.

The event started with a long song and *morin huur* ensemble and continued to include throat singing and a demonstration of both traditional dancing and contortionism. The late afternoon program also involved archery, horse racing, and a wrestling competition, which the vice president briefly joined in, facing off against a very large Mongolian wrestler in traditional dress. At one point, Vice President Biden aimed his bow in the direction of the accompanying press corps, urging them to "be careful." As with many foreign visitors, he was given a parting gift—a restive brown horse that he promptly named Celtic in honor of his Irish ancestry. After the foreign delegation had left, the gift horse was passed on to a local herder, never to be saddled or ridden again—or, at least, that is what high-level visitors are told when they inevitably ask what will become of "their" horse once they have left Mongolia.

****

High-level affirmation for Mongolia as an emerging democracy is further reflected in a series of other visits over the years, including trips to Ulaanbaatar by senior American officials from the Department of State and Department of Defense at various times. Most notably, four US secretaries of state—James Baker, Madeleine Albright, Condoleezza Rice, and Hillary Clinton—each visited Mongolia during their tenures in office. Former president Jimmy Carter has also visited Mongolia, undertaking a birding expedition to the Gobi in August 2001.

The first trip by a sitting US secretary of state to Mongolia occurred in August 1990, when James Baker visited Ulaanbaatar. As he recalls in his memoir:

> Only days before, Mongolia had completed its first multiparty elections in nearly seventy years, with a voter turnout of more than 90 percent. The revolution in Eastern Europe was slow in spreading across the Urals, but Mongolian democracy had a real chance to flourish, and I wanted to lend the moral encouragement of the United States to their efforts at self-determination.
>
> (*The Politics of Diplomacy: Revolution, War and Peace, 1989–1992*)

As fate would have it, Baker's visit occurred at exactly the same time that Saddam Hussein launched the Iraqi invasion of Kuwait, provoking an international crisis that ultimately resulted in the First Gulf War. From the very start, Baker worked to forge an international coalition against the precedent of one small country being invaded by a much larger neighbor. Indeed, Mongolia itself issued one of the first statements condemning the invasion—a gesture that Kuwait remembers with appreciation to this day and one that almost certainly played a role in Kuwait's decision in 2010 to become the first Arab country to open an embassy in Ulaanbaatar.

In Baker's recollection, the US embassy in Mongolia in August 1990 consisted of "three rooms on a stairwell in an apartment building." Communications proved difficult, and the decision was quickly made to cut short his already brief official visit and return to Washington by way of Moscow as part of an effort to also enlist Russian support.

In recalling his first visit, Baker later praised Mongolian officials for their hospitality as well as for their flexibility and support. He also committed himself to a longer second visit—a commitment he fulfilled the following year when he visited Mongolia again, this time staying longer and seeing more of the countryside.

If anything, this second visit confirmed and strengthened Baker's interest in Mongolia still further, an important factor in generating additional international support for Mongolia in various international forums during the coming months, when Russia terminated its large assistance program to Mongolia and the country's future economic prospects seemed especially bleak.

At a personal level, Baker maintained a strong interest in Mongolia even after leaving office, visiting the country in 1996 to observe elections and then again with his son in 2006 to explore possible business interests. In retrospect, it is no exaggeration to say that Baker's initial two visits to Mongolia during the early

1990s were landmark events, playing an important role in laying the foundation for a productive partnership between the United States and Mongolia that continued after he left office.

Baker is often remembered in Mongolia as one of the authors of the term "third neighbor" to describe the concept of Mongolia looking beyond its two immediate geographical neighbors to develop strong relations with the world's democratic nations, including not only the United States but also Japan, South Korea, India, Canada, Australia, and various European countries. In fact, the "third neighbor" concept now serves as one of the pillars of Mongolian foreign policy, affirming as it does the importance of maintaining positive relations with its immediate neighbors, Russia and China, while also reaching out to a range of other countries as well as the United Nations and other multilateral organizations further afield.

Secretary of State Madeleine Albright's visit in May 1998 during the Clinton administration struck similar themes while also reflecting broad, bipartisan US support for assisting Mongolia during the difficult years of its transition. She was met on arrival by her counterpart, Foreign Minister Amarjargal. From there, she proceeded directly to the countryside, visiting a herder named Vanchigdorjit living in the Jargalantin Am Valley, where she was offered both fermented mare's milk and a horse. During her brief trip, the secretary addressed the Great Hural, lauding Mongolia for its commitment to both democratic values and an open economy. She also met with President Bagabandi.

Albright's visit took place at a time of considerable political turmoil in Mongolia, Prime Minister Elbegdorj having only just assumed office. In her public remarks, she emphasized the role that both participation and effective communication can play in strengthening grassroots democracy.

As the first female US secretary of state, Albright took a special interest in the challenges facing women in Mongolia. During that May 1998 trip, she participated in a roundtable discussion with several Mongolian women, lauding their contribution as providing an "extraordinary beacon of democracy." She also announced a $30,000 grant to the National Center against Violence. Subsequently, the funds supported a domestic violence shelter in Ulaanbaatar—a facility now called the "Madeleine Albright Shelter"—that continues to provide valuable service to the women of Mongolia to this day.

As with a number of senior visitors, Madeleine Albright returned to Mongolia on a second occasion, this time as a private citizen. Her return visit to Ulaanbaatar in April 2011 evoked many memories. During the course of her stay, she gave a lecture at the Ministry of Foreign Affairs and Trade entitled "Celebrating Mongolian Democracy: A Special Role in Asia." While fondly recalling her visit to Mongolia 13 years earlier, she also reflected on both the challenges and opportunities facing Mongolia in the years ahead.

First Lady Hillary Clinton was another high-profile visitor to offer support for Mongolia's fledgling democracy during the 1990s. In her memoir *Living History*, she recalls her September 1995 trip to Ulaanbaatar fondly, noting, "We arrived on a crystal-clear day with bright sunshine" and left immediately from the airport to spend time with a herder family. She was "mesmerized" by her encounter, striving to come up with the right set of adjectives to describe the life of a traditional rural Mongolian family that had set up its fall camp against a backdrop of the steppes that was "stunning in its vastness, serenity and natural beauty." As she recalls, she also tasted fermented mare's milk when it was offered to her, though everyone in the White House press corps declined it for themselves.

"The country faced difficult times," Clinton writes in her memoirs. "It was important for the United States to show support for the Mongolian people and their elected leadership and a visit from the First Lady to one of the most remote capitals of the world was one way to do it."

For the jaded traveler, journalist, or academic who is already familiar with Mongolia and its many challenges, the inevitable references to democracy and remote but stupendous landscapes may begin to seem hackneyed and even stereotypical. Yet such comments reflect the reality that senior visitors are often truly impressed by what they encounter when they experience Mongolia for the first time, developing a real affection for the country and its people that Mongolians, as survivors throughout the centuries, have often used to their advantage. Moreover, the historical record suggests that positive impressions by first-time visitors, especially senior ones, can sometimes reap dividends for Mongolia later on. Without doubt, high-level American officials who have visited Mongolia in recent years have usually come away impressed by it.

Events on Hillary Clinton's crowded schedule during her first visit to Mongolia in the early fall of 1995 included lunch with President Ochirbat, tea with a group of Mongolian women, and a meeting with students at the Mongolian National University. In her remarks at the university, she spoke of "the courage of the Mongolian people and their leadership, urging them to continue their struggle toward democracy." The brief visit made a strong impression on Mrs. Clinton regarding Mongolia's commitment to democracy, despite the many obstacles it faced: "From then on, whenever we visited a country that was struggling to become democratic, we would break into a chorus of 'Let them come to Mongolia!' And so they should."

Nearly 17 years later—on July 9, 2012—Clinton paid a second visit to Mongolia, this time as secretary of state. The stopover was part of a 13-day worldwide tour, the longest, most complex, and most grueling of her tenure in office: prior to landing in Ulaanbaatar, she had visited France, Afghanistan, and Japan, and immediately afterwards she proceeded to Southeast Asia, stopping off for meetings and other events in Vietnam, Laos, and Cambodia, before returning to the United States via the Middle East. On several occasions during her 21-hour stopover in Mongolia, she recalled her previous admonition ("Let them come to Mongolia"), in this case congratulating Mongolia on its recent parliamentary elections in late June 2012 as part of an impressive series of electoral milestones stretching back two decades.

This time, Secretary Clinton's schedule included meetings with President Elbegdorj, Prime Minister Batbold, and Foreign Minister Zandanshatar. At the meeting with President Elbegdorj, which took place in a large ceremonial *ger* at Government House, Secretary Clinton was once again given the opportunity to politely sip fermented mare's milk. Ushered into the lavish round felt tent, the Mongolian president welcomed her warmly into "our oval office." Following the meeting, she participated in a special session of the governing council of the Community of Democracies; addressed an International Women's Leadership Forum sponsored by the Community of Democracies; officially launched the new Leaders Engaged in New Democracies (LEND) network; and met with members of the embassy staff, including families.

As with her initial visit as First Lady 17 years earlier, Secretary Clinton was able to see something of Mongolia's countryside outside Ulaanbaatar, in this case traveling by road more than an hour east to Terelj National Park, with its attractive hills, rivers, trees, and rock formations. Before flying off to Vietnam, she spent one night in Terelj relaxing by a swiftly flowing river at sunset while Assistant Secretary of State for East Asia and the Pacific Kurt Campbell enjoyed a few brief moments of fly-fishing. Amidst the headaches, heartaches, and uncertainties posed by the "Arab Spring" and problematic developments elsewhere in Asia, the stopover in Mongolia offered a welcome if momentary opportunity for relaxation and reflection beside the Terelj River in the face of a growing list of more pressing challenges in other parts of the world. By comparison, potential issues related to Mongolia seemed both more modest and more manageable.

The Mongolian journey also offered a useful opportunity to advance concerns related to the role of women, both within the region and beyond. Other participants at the Women's Leadership Forum organized in advance of the secretary's trip included former Canadian Prime Minister Kim Campbell and former Kyrgyz President Roza Otunbaeva. The former president recalled both the historical relationship between Mongolia and Kyrgyzstan (many Kyrgyz believe that their ancestors once lived in western Mongolia) and more recent ties, including the ongoing support over several years that Mongolia offered for Kyrgyzstan's struggling democracy. (President Elbegdorj had visited Bishkek earlier in the year as part of a series of continuing exchanges involving officials from the two countries.) All nine of Mongolia's recently elected female parliamentarians, spanning the entire spectrum of Mongolian politics, also attended.

The secretary's remarks at the Women's Leadership Forum, while offering encouragement for those working toward greater female participation in politics, included a broader focus on Asian democracy. Referring to Mongolia as "an inspiration and a model," she noted, "[A]gainst long odds, surrounded by powerful neighbors who had their own ideas about Mongolia's future, the Mongolian people came together with great courage to transform a one-party Communist dictatorship into a pluralistic, democratic political system." She then made the case that democracy and human rights should be viewed as "the birthright of every person born in the world."

One key section of her speech directly challenged statements made by some commentators that democracy "isn't perfectly at home in Asia" or might be "antithetical to Asian values." Citing developments in Thailand, Burma, East Timor, and elsewhere, Clinton argued that these nations "show what is possible." At the same time, she directly challenged countries that "resist reforms," specifically taking on the argument that "democracy threatens stability" or that "democracy is a privilege belonging to wealthy countries." Subsequent media reporting interpreted these sections of the speech as a subtle "dig" at China, noting that while Secretary Clinton never mentioned China by name, some of her reflections might well be relevant to Mongolia's large neighbor to the south.

As already noted, Secretary of State Condoleezza Rice accompanied President Bush during his historic visit to Mongolia in November 2005, making her the fourth American secretary of state to visit Mongolia while in office. Only a month earlier, Donald Rumsfeld had become the first and so far only US secretary of defense to visit the country. While his schedule included meetings with high-level Mongolian officials, it was clear from the outset that one of his specific purposes was to thank Mongolia for its contributions to international coalition efforts in both Afghanistan and Iraq.

This appreciation was notably reflected in Rumsfeld's meeting with some 180 Mongolian soldiers who had recently returned from service in the two war zones, sharing the danger and experience of war with American soldiers serving there. During his remarks to the Mongolian military contingent, Rumsfeld specifically singled out two Mongolian soldiers—Sergeant Azzaya and Sergeant Samuu-Yondon—for their vigilance in February 2004 while serving with a Polish detachment at Hilla in Iraq. Facing a split-second decision to determine the true intentions of an Iraqi in a pickup truck who was driving erratically outside their camp, they fired on the driver, who turned out to be a would-be suicide bomber. Their prompt and decisive action halted the attack in its tracks, thereby saving countless lives.

* * * * * * *

While high-level visits help affirm the importance of US-Mongolia bilateral relations as well as mutually shared views about democracy, US support over the years also includes a strong "grassroots" dimension, one based partly on the provision of both moral and material support to Mongolian civil society. As noted earlier, such aid has come from many sources, including the Asia Foundation, International Republican Institute, National Democratic Institute, and National Endowment for Democracy. While USAID has been at the forefront of such efforts, direct grants have also been provided through the US embassy, in part to address issues such as trafficking, child labor, media, and disability concerns.

Regardless of the specific activity being supported, there was widespread interest on the part of the international NGO community in building and strengthening Mongolia's indigenous NGO sector and making it more transparent. American and international NGOs played a part in many of these programs. Indeed, the growth of Mongolia's NGO sector and civil society over the past two decades is in no small measure linked to the early initiatives launched by many of these organizations, some of which have received US government funding but many of which rely primarily on private donations from ordinary American citizens.

The emergence of trafficking as an issue reflects one of the more negative aspects of globalization, namely the dubious movement of people—sometimes via forced labor, often including vulnerable young women—to other countries, where they are all too often abused and exploited. In the case of Mongolia, such concerns include the trafficking of young women to various Asian destinations, including China, Korea, Japan, and Malaysia. As Mongolia's mining boom unfolds, it is possible that Mongolia will itself become a trafficking destination. One of the hallmarks of democracy anywhere is the willingness to talk about problems and address them openly, rather than ignore them or pretend that they do not exist. In the case of trafficking, the US embassy has worked with civil society over many years to proactively address these concerns and minimize their impact before they become a much bigger problem.

In recognition of these ongoing efforts worldwide, the US Department of State each year honors several individuals with "TIP Hero" awards, giving them to those who have made a notable impact on addressing Trafficking in Persons (TIP) concerns. As a reflection of the commitment of individual Mongolians to addressing these concerns, two Mongolians have received such awards in recent years, including the "TIP Hero" award issued in 2010 to Geleg Ganbayasgakh for her work with the Gender Equality Center, which so far has assisted some 300 trafficking victims, in part through its phone hotline, counseling, and shelters.

Ms. Ganbayasgakh has herself designed university curricula, textbooks, and pamphlets on the nature of human trafficking and approaches towards ending it. Reflecting a long-standing interest in issues affecting women, the award—signed by Secretary of State Hillary Clinton—was delivered in person by former Secretary of State Madeleine Albright at the US ambassador's residence during a private visit to Ulaanbaatar in April 2011.

Disability issues in Mongolia have also received increased attention from the US embassy, reflecting the view that one of the core strengths of democracy is its ability to provide a "voice" to individuals and communities that all too often have almost no chance to be heard. Already, there is a growing interest on the part of Mongolians with disabled children and adult Mongolians who are blind, deaf, or otherwise disabled to participate more fully in the economic, political, and social life of the country—an interest which the US embassy actively seeks to support.

Building on this interest, USAID programs implemented since 2009 include several activities related specifically to disabled people. While engaging with local NGOs working with Mongolia's disabled population, the program also aims at effecting policy change, including the adoption of regulations to ensure that new buildings provide access for Mongolians confined to wheelchairs. In advance of the 2012 parliamentary elections, the USAID-funded NGO Mercy Corps provided support aimed at ensuring that disabled Mongolians have access to voting booths.

A variety of other US embassy outreach programs have strengthened engagement with Mongolia's disabled population in other ways. For example, nearly every cultural event sponsored by the US embassy in recent years has included outreach focused on Mongolia's disabled community. In addition, the alumni association of USG-funded students who have studied in the United States has organized summer camps for disabled Mongolians and supported events to publicize disability concerns among the broader Mongolian public.

In September 2010, Andrew Imparato, president and CEO of the American Association of People with Disabilities, based in Washington, D.C., visited Mongolia to discuss, among other issues, aspects of the American Disabilities Act that might be relevant in Mongolia.

Following that visit, the Mongolian NGO "Wind Bird" sponsored a unique, two-week study trip to the United States that included meetings with Special Assistant to the President for Disability Policy Kareem Dale and State Department Special Advisor for International Disability Rights Judith Heumann. In addition, the group—which included both journalists and disabled people—saw at first hand various US approaches to disability issues in Washington, Baltimore, and Seattle. In their own words, participants returned "inspired" and "motivated" to adapt to Mongolia some "lessons learned" from their trip across the United States.

****

International partnerships between countries do not necessarily imply identical views on the issues of the day. Indeed, voting patterns for Mongolia and the United States at times differ in the United Nations and in other international forums. However, the relationship and level of trust is such that American and Mongolian diplomats freely and candidly discuss a range of issues, even on occasions when their views and perspectives may diverge. Yet it is often the case that Mongolia and the United States find common ground on a number of important issues and concerns.

For example, in 2010 and again in 2011 during its tenure on the board of governors at the International Atomic Energy Agency (IAEA) in Vienna, Mongolian and American diplomats regularly discussed a wide range of issues, including shared concerns about nuclear proliferation related to Iran. Similarly, during the first half of 2011, the United States along with a number of other countries participated in an ongoing dialogue with Mongolia, privately expressing concern about Syria's pending 2012 bid to become a member of the UN Commission on Human Rights at a time when hundreds of Syrians were already being killed on city streets across the country. In the end, Mongolia indicated that it was willing to consider putting itself forward for a vacant seat on the Commission if no other Asian country would do so—a step that, by some accounts, was sufficient for Syria to withdraw its candidacy and cede its prospective seat on the Commission to another Arab country, Kuwait.

Historically, Mongolia has had long-standing ties with North Korea. More recently, it has forged robust ties with South Korea as well, potentially putting it in a position to at some point provide a "bridge" between two very different political and economic systems. Although Mongolia's own efforts in this area have not yet borne fruit, it has on occasion suggested that its example might one day be relevant to North Korea, especially its experience in moving relatively quickly from a Soviet-style political and economic system to a market-oriented one following its "decision for democracy" just over two decades ago. In the words of former deputy secretary of state Richard Armitage, it is useful and appropriate for Mongolia to keep lines of connection with both Koreas "warm," in the hopes that it might one day help facilitate useful and ultimately broad-based changes that contribute to stability across the Korean peninsula.

****

Mongolia's assumption of the chairmanship of the Community of Democracies in July 2011 seemed especially appropriate, representing another important milestone in Mongolia's ongoing journey as a country committed to democracy. At the same time, it provided further opportunity for a continued conversation on democratic issues between the United States and Mongolia, a conversation that began at the outset of Mongolia's "Democratic Revolution" in the early 1990s. In this high-profile position, Mongolia has already engaged with other countries such as Tunisia, Burma (Myanmar), and Kyrgyzstan on how its own experience with democracy may be relevant elsewhere.

The idea of the Community of Democracies first emerged in 1999 when Madeleine Albright was secretary of state. The Community itself was officially organized in Warsaw in June 2000, resulting in a "Warsaw Declaration" that emphasized the importance of elections, freedom of expression, education, rule of law, and peaceful assembly as true hallmarks of democracy everywhere. Ten countries were represented at a ministerial level at that first meeting—Chile, the Czech Republic, India, Mali, Mexico, Poland, Portugal, South Africa, South Korea, and the United States.

Six years later, the convening group added six more countries—including not only Mongolia, but also Cape Verde, El Salvador, Italy, Morocco, and the Philippines—to its membership. Prior to Mongolia's chairmanship, previous chairs included Poland, South Korea, Chile, Mali, Portugal, and Lithuania. The rationale behind the establishment of the Community of Democracies reflects a recognition that liberty and democracy will always be subject to challenge and can never be taken for granted. As an organization, the Community explicitly acknowledges the importance of civil society and encourages its active participation.

Even before assuming its two-year chairmanship in July 2011, Mongolian officials had noted that during their term in office they wished to emphasize democratic education and civil society as important themes, culminating in hosting the biennial Community of Democracies Ministerial Summit. As already noted, during its chairmanship Mongolia welcomed Secretary of State Clinton to Mongolia in early July 2012 to participate in a special session of the governing council, launch the LEND initiative, and address the International Women's Leadership Forum. Other international events held in Ulaanbaatar during the country's term as head of the Community of Democracies included a seminar on "Education for Democracy" (May 2012) and a meeting on "Election Challenges in a Young Democracy" (November 2012). For Mongolia, its time in a leading role was to culminate in the Ministerial Summit in Ulaanbaatar in late April 2013--after which the chairmanship would pass to another young democracy, El Salvador.

A few skeptical outside observers have on occasion suggested that Mongolia's interest in democracy is only superficial, reflecting little more than a foreign policy ploy aimed at setting Mongolia apart from its neighbors in Central and Northeast Asia in the eyes of the rest of the world and thereby garnering more international interest and support than would otherwise be the case. But, so far, Mongolia's commitment to democracy has been widely accepted within the country over two decades, despite growing cynicism about politicians, deep concern about corruption, and an often vociferous debate about what a mining-based economy portends for Mongolia's future.

* * * * * * *

Looking back over the course of two decades, democracy in Mongolia, as in other countries, is primarily a continuing journey rather than a final destination. It is a journey with many bumps, obstacles, detours, and hurdles at every step of the way. This was highlighted in April 2012 with the arrest on corruption charges of former president, prime minister, and speaker Enkhbayar, a leading figure from the Mongolian People's Revolutionary Party (MPRP) who had dominated Mongolian politics for much of the 2000s.

As the international community watched events unfold, early comments emphasized the importance of adherence to transparency, rule of law, and due process, even while the Mongolian legal process took its course. Concerns were also expressed in some quarters, both locally and abroad, that the timing of the arrest was politically motivated and primarily aimed at excluding Enkhbayar from running in the parliamentary elections scheduled for late June 2012. These concerns were further heightened when Enkhbayar went on an extended hunger strike that appeared to threaten his health and attracted additional attention in Mongolia and abroad. They gained still more momentum when Mongolia's General Election Commission (GEC) disqualified Enkhbayar from being a candidate in June 2012, not long before the elections were due to commence.

Public opinion on the case was and remains divided, even after Enkhbayar was convicted of corruption and sentenced to a four-year prison term in July 2012. Here again, televised scenes involving the undignified arrest of a former president—followed weeks later by his exclusion from the June elections—contributed to a sense of uncertainty and concern about what these developments might mean for the future of democracy in Mongolia.

The former president's international outreach campaign went into especially high gear during late spring and early summer 2012, convincing a number of highly placed individuals from the United States, Australia, and Britain to launch an intense lobbying effort of their own on behalf of Enkhbayar to demonstrate that his case might mark the demise of democracy in Mongolia. Those actually living in Mongolia were less convinced. Subsequently, the annual Freedom House survey, issued in early 2013, registered an improvement in Mongolia's rankings. In continuing to describe it as a "free" country, the Freedom House report assigned Mongolia a 1 on political freedom (including the conduct of free and fair elections) and a 2 on civil society, on a scale of 1 to 7, with 1 reflecting the highest mark possible. This put Mongolia in the same place as Croatia, Ghana, Hungary, Israel, Japan, and South Korea and far ahead of its two immediate neighbors, Russia and China, and the five nearby "stans" of former Soviet Central Asia (Kazakhstan, Kyrgyzstan, Turkmenistan, Uzbekistan, and Tajikistan). Mongolia's ranking in Transparency International's annual corruption index also improved during the same period, moving from a low point of 120th out of 182 in 2011 to 94th out of 174 in 2012, placing it on par with countries such as India and Senegal.

As the Enkhbayar case gained momentum and headlines during May and June 2012, other commentators as well as the "blogosphere" highlighted the corrosive effects of corruption, arguing that no one, least of all senior politicians, including former presidents and prime ministers, should ever be above the law. A number of Mongolians went even further in their comments, suggesting that the most strident international criticism directed toward Mongolia at a time when it finally seemed to be taking corruption seriously was unwarranted and even hypocritical, especially when it came from wealthy foreigners with powerful political connections of their own. According to such critics, it was precisely this unhealthy mix of wealth, economic interests, connections, access, and political power that, increasingly, seemed to be undermining democracy in Mongolia.

Whatever the merits of the case, Mongolians across the country voted in large numbers in parliamentary elections held on June 28, 2012, reflecting yet again the propensity on the part of the Mongolian voting public to surprise. About two-thirds of those eligible actually voted, down from the 90 percent or more that went to the polls in earlier elections back in the 1990s and early 2000s, but still a respectable figure when compared with the turnout for most elections in Europe and North America.

When all the votes were counted, the Democratic Party (DP), tracing its origins to coalitions formed during the early years of Mongolia's democracy movement, held the most seats, though not enough to form a new government on its own. The Mongolian People's Party (MPP), the country's oldest political party dating back to the Soviet era, placed second. Enkhbayar's breakaway party—which assumed the mantle of the old Mongolian People's Revolution Party (MPRP) while also forming a temporary "Justice" coalition with the Mongolian National Democratic Party (MNDP)—came third, garnering more than 20 percent of the popular vote and emerging as a potential "kingmaker" in forming the next government. While the MPRP/MNDP Justice platform argued for a strongly nationalistic economic policy, individual party members affirmed a continued commitment to maintaining and promoting strong ties with Mongolia's various "third neighbors," including the United States. Other political parties also shared this view.

My assignment as US ambassador to Mongolia concluded in July 2012, providing me an opportunity to watch the June 2012 elections firsthand just prior to leaving Mongolia for a new posting in Afghanistan.

On the eve of elections, taking the long but scenic journey on dirt tracks through the Hangai Mountains from Bayanhongor north to Tsetsergleg, I talked to GEC officials at small polling stations in isolated valleys or on mountain ridges with breathtaking views toward the sparkling rivers and deep green forests below. In each case, the relevant staff expressed confidence that the elections scheduled for the next day would be successful, despite their having to become familiar with a new election law that introduced a measure of proportional representation as well as the use of electronic voting machines for the first time.

On the following day, I got up early to watch the polls open in a gymnasium in Tsetserleg, capital of Arkhangai. Appropriately, I was asked to produce my "monitoring pass" from the Mongolian Ministry of Foreign Affairs and Trade before being permitted to enter. Monitors from all the major political parties had registered ahead of me, intending to watch closely throughout the day as the electoral process took its course. About 30 people were already lined up to be among the first to vote.

Just before 7 a.m., the GEC official responsible for the polling station made a few brief remarks to open the proceedings. Then everyone—GEC officials, election monitors, and voters alike—stood at attention, hands over their hearts, to listen to their stirring national anthem. Many of the early voters were elderly and most of the women wore traditional *deels*, lending a note of dignity as well as color to polling day, while also suggesting that Mongolians continue to regard the opportunity to cast a meaningful ballot as representing something special.

Throughout the course of the day, I observed voting at polling stations in three other provinces—Ovorhangai, Bulgan, and Tov—before reaching Ulaanbaatar by late afternoon. The scenes were impressive at each stop along the way. Outside the Erdene Zuu Monastery at Kharkorin, three women stated that they had already voted, pronouncing that the new electronic voting machines were "simple" and "easy to use." Two grizzled herders in Bulgan, wearing black leather boots and tan *deels* and burned deep brown by the sun, expressed the same sentiment before mounting their horses to ride ten miles south toward their summer camp. These were Mongolia's seventh successful parliamentary elections in succession, a rare achievement in a part of the world where such elections are more often the exception rather than the rule.

Inevitably, concern was expressed in some quarters about some of the procedural aspects of the June 2012 elections, especially among certain aspiring members of parliament who failed to get elected. In reality, though, Mongolia—and most especially individual Mongolians from the length and breadth of the country—had once again demonstrated the country's ongoing commitment to democracy, despite the obstacles. In doing so, they reflected in a visible, practical way the sentiment expressed by the young democratic leader S. Zorig, known at the time within Mongolia as the "Golden Magpie of Democracy."

Zorig's words come from a letter he had written from Moscow during the 1980s, long before his all-too-early death at the age of 36 in October 1998, when he was murdered in his Ulaanbaatar apartment, literally, according to some reports, on the eve of becoming Mongolia's youngest prime minister. Addressed to his sister Oyun, then living in Prague but later a member of parliament and government minister herself, he stated that, ultimately, he would always place his trust in the "wisdom of the Mongolian people." Years later, his statement remains as relevant as ever, perhaps offering inspiration to a new generation of Mongolians as they confront enormous challenges from every direction in the years ahead.

Chapter 4

Partnering on Development

> *"Without USAID and assistance from American companies in the energy sector, they simply would not have survived the winter of 1992–93 with an operating heating system."*

The United States Agency for International Development (USAID) launched its first program in Mongolia in November 1991, almost five years after the official opening of bilateral relations between the two countries. More than two decades later, US assistance programs continue to promote useful partnerships between the United States and Mongolia, as rapid expansion in the country's mining sector is dramatically changing Mongolia's economic prospects for the future.

During the period 1991 through 2011, the total USAID grant funding to Mongolia exceeded $220 million, with approximately half of this amount for economic growth. A further $31 million has been targeted on democracy and good governance. Additional funding allocations include $48 million for emergency energy assistance during the 1990s and $5 million on emergency food and disaster assistance, primarily in the 1990s. Apart from emergency relief, specific areas of USAID interest over the years have included small business development, financial sector reform, rural development, and environmental concerns.

Cash transfers have figured into the aid equation only rarely, although USAID did provide $10 million directly to Mongolia in 1991, when the country was struggling with the sudden cutting off of Soviet aid. It also provided another $10 million cash grant in 2009, following the global financial crisis. Remaining USAID grant allocations to Mongolia have largely been allocated on a project basis and have covered a number of areas, including several environmental activities.

Overall USAID funding levels to Mongolia over the past two decades have been relatively modest, averaging around $10 million annually, lower than that of other bilateral donors such as Japan and Germany during that same period and much lower than that of international financial institutions such as the World Bank, Asian Development Bank, and European Bank for Reconstruction and Development (EBRD). Focused assistance combined with good relations with key partners have assured a significant impact in some sectors.

In addition, other US departments and agencies have forged effective partnerships with Mongolian individuals and institutions over the years—starting with the US Department of Agriculture (USDA), but also including the Departments of Treasury, Energy, Interior, and Labor, the National Science Foundation (NSF), and the National Institutes of Health (NIH).

In particular, USDA programs have funded research and supported rural development, while Treasury programs provide technical advice to major Mongolian institutions such as the Ministry of Finance and Central Bank. The NSF and NIH support partnerships of Mongolians and Americans that aim to research and better understand a variety of health and environmental concerns. In December 2010, Colorado State University received a $1.5 million NSF grant to study the impact of climate change on Mongolian pastoralists.

The launch of a Millennium Challenge Corporation (MCC) program in Mongolia in September 2008 more than doubled US assistance levels to Mongolia while also introducing new approaches that have further strengthened the US-Mongolian development partnership. The MCC is itself an innovative concept, developed to support countries that have demonstrated a commitment in three essential areas—market-led economic growth, good governance, and investments in people. As one of the first countries to qualify for MCC funding worldwide, Mongolia effectively demonstrated its performance and commitment in all three areas. At this point, the MCC program in Mongolia is valued at $285 million in grant funds over five years and is scheduled to conclude in September 2013.

* * * * * * *

In the beginning, USAID programs in Mongolia concentrated largely on short-term emergency relief, while also providing modest assistance to help build and strengthen democracy. Launched against a backdrop of economic collapse and uncertainty following the withdrawal almost overnight of Soviet assistance during the early 1990s, the intent was simply to provide the supplies and equipment needed to keep major power plants running and buy critically needed materials, equipment, and supplies.

The initial USAID effort during late 1991 and early 1992 reflected this focus and consisted of a $10 million cash transfer and $2 million in equipment and training. The next year's program retained a similar focus, stressing the emergency response needed to shore up Mongolia's rapidly decaying energy infrastructure. By 1998, USAID had provided nearly $50 million in supplies, equipment, and technical assistance to strengthen and sustain Mongolia's crucially important power plants. Other early programs emphasized health and emergency food supplies, including funding to buy 30,000 metric tons of wheat.

Documents from that difficult period underscore just how far Mongolia has come in recent years. Looming disaster in the energy sector represented a special concern. Real fears were voiced in early USAID planning documents and embassy cables that Ulaanbaatar's power system might simply collapse: "A system breakdown in winter, even for a relatively short period of time, could be disastrous, perhaps forcing the evacuation of an estimated 50 percent of the urban population and threatening the lives of thousands of individuals."

Ambassador Lake described the situation in even more vivid terms: "The vision that hung over our heads was that in January when it's 40 below, you face a collapse of the heating system. Roughly 40 percent of the people in Ulaanbaatar, a city of half a million, would be exposed to 40 below weather with no form of heat."

Given this bleak assessment, it is not surprising that the lion's share of USAID assistance during the early 1990s was emergency and short term in nature. This required improvements not only in the main power plant but also at the coal mine in nearby Baganuur that kept it running. Both the power plant and the coal mine had been constructed during the Soviet era, and the spare parts needed to maintain operations typically had to be procured from Russia. This in turn required the tiny USAID staff based in Ulaanbaatar to prepare complicated waivers, permitting the purchase of equipment made in Russia rather than in the United States. Nonetheless, every obstacle was surmounted and Ulaanbaatar's heating system remained intact. According to Ambassador Lake, "Without USAID and assistance from American companies in the energy sector, they simply would not have survived the winter in 1992–93 with an operating [intact] heating system."

****

Even in a time of dire economic hardship, senior Mongolian officials expressed interest in building democracy and beginning a dialogue with international partners on more long-term development concerns. It was in 1990 that the Mongolian Mission to the United Nations initially approached the San Francisco-based Asia Foundation to seek assistance for the political and economic transition that was already beginning to unfold. The Asia Foundation responded positively, first with its own private funds and then, in 1991, when it received its first direct USAID grant to work in Mongolia. In that same year, it opened a resident office in Ulaanbaatar, among the first of any foreign NGO to do so.

Along with other international organizations such as the Konrad Adenauer Foundation and the Open Society Institute, the Asia Foundation quickly became an important development partner. Early programs dealt with training, technical assistance, and international exposure for a country that had been isolated for decades and even centuries. Hundreds of Mongolians participated in in-country seminars and workshops, and dozens received their first opportunity to travel abroad to Western countries through tailor-made study tours designed to bring international experience to bear on Mongolia-specific issues and concerns.

Although USAID's initial work focused heavily on the parliament and the judiciary, early democracy programs sponsored by the Asia Foundation, the International Republican Institute, and others also helped build Mongolia's nascent civil society. Indeed, small grants provided to local organizations under various USAID-funded initiatives during the 1990s included a long list of new and emerging Mongolian NGOs, such as the Center for Citizenship Education, the Center for Human Rights and Social Studies, the Consumer Foundation, the Consumer Protection Association, the Free and Democratic Journalists Association, the Liberal Women's Brain Pool, the Mongolian Association for the Conservation of Nature and Environment, the Mongolian Chamber of Commerce and Industry, the Political Education Academy, the Press Institute of Mongolia, the Women Lawyers' Association, the Women Economists' Club, the

Women's Research and Information Center, Women for Social Progress, and the Young Leaders' Club, among many others.

While direct funding for local NGOs has become more limited in recent years, there is little doubt that USAID—along with other international donors—played an important role in building and strengthening Mongolia's civil society at a time when even the basic idea of "civil society" was entirely new.

* * * * * * *

Gradually, USAID-funded activity in Mongolia began to move away from a short-term emergency relief response toward a program that was better positioned to address long-term economic concerns. These efforts gained new momentum after national elections in June 1996 placed a Democratic Party (DP) government in power, one that had voiced a strong commitment to far-ranging economic reform and placed Mongolia on an irrevocable path toward a market-based economy.

Soon after the 1996 elections, three Mongolian economists associated with a USAID-funded technical advisory project were asked to serve as economic advisors to the new DP government, one of whom became a senior economic advisor. An early USAID-supported conference held at the Mongolian government's request not long after the elections made international perspectives from Poland, Russia, Estonia, and elsewhere available to Mongolian policy makers, again with a view toward providing Mongolia with an opportunity to benefit from the experience of other former communist countries facing similar problems. Such programs helped pave the way for a period of far-reaching economic reform that put Mongolia firmly on the path toward a market-based economy.

Throughout the late 1990s and beyond, these efforts deepened the reform process in several areas, including energy, banking, tourism, trade, and privatization. Typically, USAID-funded technical advice as well as tailor-made study tours abroad involved a wide range of relevant sources, not only the United States.

For example, the ongoing USAID-funded dialogue on public administration involved a visit and presentations by a senior expert from New Zealand. Similarly, discussions on privatization drew on experience from Bulgaria, while USAID-funded energy programs included the provision of Hungarian expertise.

At the same time, these programs enabled Mongolian experts to travel abroad and interact with counterparts facing similar issues, including in countries with a shared Soviet past. More recently, USAID-funded technical assistance and training has worked closely with both government officials and the private sector to address tax reform, launch a credit bureau, establish Mongolia's Energy Regulatory Authority (ERA), introduce new approaches to mortgage financing, and improve corporate governance.

****

Policy reform can be vital in shaping new approaches and introducing significant economic change. However, it also often tends to be a very "abstract" concept, hard to grasp and seemingly removed from the day-to-day realities of individuals facing harsh economic circumstances.

For Mongolians, the challenges were especially acute in the immediate aftermath of the sudden cut-off of Soviet assistance at the beginning of the 1990s, assistance that at one point had represented 30 percent or more of Mongolia's gross domestic product (GDP). On the eve of Mongolia's democratic era, government expenditure also accounted for 65 percent of annual GDP, while the burden of external debt owed to the Soviet Union and its allies exceeded Mongolia's annual GDP by nearly 500 percent. The gap between what the country produced and what it consumed—largely on a subsidized basis from the Soviet Union—was both large and growing fast.

The phrase "shock therapy" is sometimes used to describe the policies that Mongolia adopted during the 1990s, featuring among other prescriptions a move toward market-based pricing as well as rapid privatization. Several critiques written during the early 2000s by Western academics who occasionally paid brief visits to Mongolia and sometimes took an optimistic and even credulous view of statistics generated during the Soviet period describe a never-ending series of economic disasters that left nothing but destruction in their wake. For example, one Norwegian academic referred to the country's "permanent trade deficit," as if Mongolia did not already have such deficits throughout most of the Soviet period. Similarly, he lamented the fact that a "huge share of GDP" had "permanently disappeared." The volume providing this bleak assessment was published in 2004, just as Mongolia was about to embark on a five-year period

(2004–08) in which GDP growth averaged more than 9 percent annually. Such assessments typically predicted dismal and unrelenting failure for Mongolia in the years ahead.

Although much less remarked upon in the literature, the reality is that Mongolia faced two unexpected "shocks" during the early 1990s. These shocks occurred in rapid succession and both had far-reaching impacts across Mongolia's struggling economy. The result was a deep recession that took at least a decade to recover from.

The first, and in some respects most dramatic shock that Mongolia experienced during the post-Soviet period, started with the abrupt cut-off of virtually all Russian assistance, accompanied by the demand that previously heavily subsidized products from the Soviet Union now be paid for in hard currency. This shock had little if anything to do with policy decisions available to government officials in Ulaanbaatar. On the contrary, it was the economic implosion that followed the Soviet departure that constituted the first big shock, making current approaches untenable and causing Mongolia to seek both financial and technical assistance from abroad.

For the Government of Mongolia, the cupboard was literally bare: it had almost no hard currency and few immediate prospects of earning any. Moreover, it lacked the means and the budget to maintain the heavy subsidies of state-owned enterprises that had been a hallmark of Mongolia's economic policy during previous decades.

For Mongolian officials at the time, the situation and the range of available choices differed from those confronting Russian policy makers following the breakup of the Soviet Union, a "closed economy," subsidized in significant part by the largest constituent republic (Russia), even as Russia also benefitted from access to the natural resources and other products provided by the outlying republics. The emergence out of the debris of the Soviet empire of newly independent countries—Ukraine, Belarus, Moldova, Armenia, Georgia, Azerbaijan, Latvia, Lithuania, Estonia, Kazakhstan, Kyrgyzstan, Uzbekistan, Turkmenistan, and Tajikistan—was highly disruptive and quickly set in motion a complex series of new economic relationships.

However, Russia as the core "successor" state to what had once been the Soviet Union did at least inherit a manufacturing base as well as a large and potentially self-sufficient economy, one that included a fairly significant internal market numbering more than 140 million consumers, along with several actual and potential sources of foreign exchange. While facing hard choices, policy makers in a newly independent Russia could therefore contemplate several plausible alternate development strategies when setting a course forward. The new Russian economy may have faced severe economic distortions, but at least it did not depend entirely on subsidies from an external power in order to survive.

In contrast, the entire Mongolian economy had been artificially kept afloat for many years by subsidies from the Soviet Union, subsidies that were eliminated almost overnight. In addition, its population numbered considerably less than three million, representing a tiny domestic market. Perhaps not surprisingly, its workforce produced little in the way of either consumer goods or machinery and other heavy equipment. Mongolia's infrastructure was also woefully inadequate, having less than 1,000 miles of paved road in a country the size of Western Europe.

For Mongolia, it was not a question of reallocating budgets or redirecting investment within the parameters of a large, existing, and stand-alone economy that had already achieved some measure of self-sufficiency and conceivably might have made a rational choice to "go it alone." Rather, Mongolia at the beginning of the 1990s was an extraordinarily aid-dependent country, suddenly cut loose from all previous sources of capital and investment and with little hope of finding alternative options to replace them. As one of the most aid-dependent countries on the planet, it could no longer maintain and sustain a Soviet-style welfare state, even had its politicians and public wanted to.

Against this backdrop, Mongolia's economic future appeared to hinge on the introduction of a new and very different market-based approach based on policy reforms that carried with them a second round of "shocks," in this case involving market-based pricing mechanisms, large-scale privatizations, and a vastly expanded role for the private sector.

Relatively quickly, Mongolia became just as dependent on the international donor community as it had been on the Soviet Union. Indeed, for most of the 1990s and into the early 2000s, foreign assistance represented approximately 30 percent of GDP, just as it had during the 1980s when the Soviet Union had been Mongolia's chief benefactor. Unlike the 1980s, assistance during the 1990s came from many sources and reflected a range of different perspectives, all of them broadly sympathetic to free market approaches while disagreeing on the details on how to get there.

Privately funded NGOs provided additional assistance, to some extent offering a modest "safety net" at a time when Mongolia's own economy was rapidly imploding. For example, for most of the 1990s and into the first decade of the 2000s the annual budget of the international NGO World Vision exceeded that of USAID, with much of the World Vision budget based on child sponsorships from individual donors in Hong Kong, Japan, Singapore, South Korea, and other Asian countries. Many smaller NGOs also became involved at a time when individual Mongolians often faced extraordinarily difficult social and economic circumstances.

International donor gatherings in Ulaanbaatar, Tokyo, and elsewhere emphasized the importance of aid co-ordination. However, in reality senior Mongolian policy makers had to weigh a flood of advice, some of it conflicting, from a range of donors that included bilateral country aid programs (notably, Japan, Germany, Korea, and the United States), international financial institutions (the International Monetary Fund, the Asian Development Bank, the World Bank, and, later, the European Bank for Reconstruction and Development), various UN agencies, and a broad spectrum of NGOs.

Rather than following any straight-line trajectory or reflecting any single "pure" point of view, policy decisions varied throughout the decade and beyond, depending on election results, the views of particular politicians, and economic circumstances prevailing at the time, both globally and within Mongolia. Mongolian policy makers followed some of the advice proffered but rejected much of it, choosing a path that involved many twists and turns, as well as occasional detours and false starts. As in any democracy, different governments emphasized different themes, though all of them affirmed broad support for a policy of market-oriented economic growth that reflected a decisive rejection of the country's Soviet past.

USAID was a part of the international donor mix throughout the 1990s and into the 2000s but by no means the only part. Attempts were made to focus USAID technical assistance in a few areas, most notably energy, the financial sector, some aspects of privatization, and, later, the tax system. In addition,

USAID made a concerted effort to introduce Mongolian officials to the experience of other countries weighing similar choices, especially within the former Soviet Union and among the newly emerging nations of Central and Eastern Europe.

By the early 2000s, the proportion of Mongolia's GDP represented by the private sector had grown from almost nothing to more than 75 percent. Leaders from across the political spectrum supported the broad outlines of this transformation, while disagreeing, sometimes strongly, on the details. While Mongolia experienced continuous economic decline throughout most of the 1990s, by the early 2000s the first signs of sustained economic growth in GDP were also finally beginning to appear.

Despite the obvious challenges faced in turning around a battered economy with minimal infrastructure, bankrupt state-owned companies, huge debts, and large financing gaps, some drew encouragement from the findings of the Mongolian pollster L. Sumati and others which repeatedly and consistently suggested that, while Mongolians faced difficult economic circumstances, worried about corruption, and had become skeptical about their politicians, there was widespread consensus across society that the country had made the "right choice" when it embarked on a new, and at times difficult and demanding, economic and political path at the start of the 1990s. Indeed, routinely and over many years throughout the late 1990s and early 2000s, more than 80 percent of Mongolians affirmed the decision to embark on the path of a market economy and more than 90 percent supported the country's decision to follow democracy.

While views on the mechanisms chosen to transform Mongolia into a market-based economy during the 1990s and into the 2000s vary, the reality is that the country is now in a very different place than it was in 1990 or even in 2000. The far-reaching impact of the rapid withdrawal of Soviet assistance followed by the quick introduction of market-led, private-sector-driven economic policies continue to reverberate. Issues of corruption, inequality, and poverty very much remain on Mongolia's development agenda, though the tools used to measure and assess the magnitude of these issues remain notoriously unreliable. In addition, as Mongolia develops its mining resources, it is experiencing at first hand the challenges of mineral-rich economies everywhere, including the specter of "Dutch disease" and the high degree of currency appreciation and rapid inflation that usually accompanies it. At the same time, Mongolians have welcomed many of the changes that have taken place since 1990, most especially in their ability to travel, acquire property, make personal choices about how to live their lives, benefit from the fruits of their own labor, and attain access to consumer goods unheard of two decades ago.

Looking ahead, international experience from mining-based economies in other parts of the world offers a number of sobering "lessons learned." Among other things, this international experience typically emphasizes the corrosive effects of corruption; the importance of good governance; the need to invest in education; the imperative to improve infrastructure; the utility of avoiding a one-dimensional, "mining only" economy; and the importance of effectively addressing environmental concerns. Already, Mongolian officials have visited some of the more successful mineral-based economies, including Botswana, Chile, and Norway. They have also looked into some of the experience available in the United States, including that offered by the Alaska Fund. While drawing on that experience and looking for ways to apply it in Mongolia, the central challenge remains as daunting as ever—effective implementation.

****

My own introduction to the formidable list of development challenges facing Mongolia came in August 2001 when I arrived in Ulaanbaatar to take up my new three-year assignment as USAID mission director, assuming responsibility for a $10 million annual program budget and a five person office with one American (myself), three Mongolian professional staff, and a driver.

The Mongolian GDP for that year (2001) was estimated at approximately $1.1 billion, the state budget at just over $430 million. Foreign aid, estimated to be in the $250–$300 million range annually for much of the 1990s and early 2000s, represented approximately 30 percent of GDP, just as it had during the Soviet era. Direct foreign investment was around $43 million, a trivial amount.

These figures stand in stark contrast to 2012, little more than a decade later, when Mongolia's GDP was estimated to have reached $10 billion; the state budget stood at $4 billion; and foreign aid, while remaining on the order of $300 million annually, now represented less than 4 percent of GDP. Direct foreign investment had increased exponentially and by now easily exceeded $1 billion.

Other contrasts are just as startling. For example, in the early 2000s, a UNDP report described Mongolia as one of the five "most aid dependent" countries in the world and saw little hope that the situation would improve anytime soon. Yet by the early 2010s, Mongolia was routinely ranked in international publications as one of the world's fastest-growing economies, in turn leading to rapid growth in both per capita GDP and per capita income. As a result, the relative importance of foreign aid to Mongolia has vastly diminished. While donor assistance still has a role to play in Mongolia, it is much less important in the broader scheme of things than was the case one or two decades earlier.

In recent years, rapid economic growth in Mongolia has been accompanied by increasing concerns about corruption, both actual and perceived. For example, in the early 2000s Mongolia ranked in the "bottom 50 percent" in the annual corruption rankings produced by Transparency International—half the countries included in the tables were "better" than Mongolia in this ranking, but half were also "worse." Unfortunately, as noted earlier, Mongolia's position in the Transparency International tables slipped markedly through 2011, when it dropped to 120 out of the 182 countries surveyed. While the Transparency International survey for 2012 indicated a modest if welcome improvement (Mongolia moved to 94 out of the 174 countries surveyed for that year), Mongolia still has much work to do in addressing a number of persistent corruption concerns.

At the same time, most leading social indicators in Mongolia have improved—in some cases, significantly—since the early 1990s. Accurate figures over an extended period of time are not always reliable. As reported by the World Bank, the life expectancy for a Mongolian at birth in 1990 was estimated at just over 60 years--nearly 58 for men and just over 63 for women (some sources put them at somewhat higher levels). By 2010, the comparable figures had climbed to nearly 68 years (64 for men, 72 for women).

Among other things, these figures reflect significant improvements in Mongolia's maternal, child, and infant mortality rates during the post-Soviet era, led partly by improvements in vaccination coverage that are now approaching 100 percent. Noncommunicable diseases are now the leading cause of death in Mongolia, reflecting a health profile that is more like a West European nation rather than a traditional "developing" country. While overall government spending for the health sector has declined as a proportion of total public spending, economic growth means that the total amount available for both public and private health spending is much greater than ever before.

These same trends are apparent in education. For example, in 1990 the World Bank reported that Mongolia devoted 17.62 percent of its annual government expenditures to education, a proportion that fell to 14.61 percent in 2009. At the same time, considerably more resources than ever before are available for education, largely because of increased tax collection and rapid economic growth. Improvements have also been registered in the pupil-teacher ratio for both primary and secondary school. Overall, the number of primary students in Mongolia increased from 165,400 in 1990 to 273,966 in 2010. The number of Mongolians enrolled in college or university also increased dramatically during the same period.

Some critics have argued that Mongolia's decision to embark on a market-led economic path has resulted in a downsized government, with a diminished role for the public sector. In reality, tax revenues in Mongolia have increased tremendously over the last two decades, and the country now has far more financial resources available for health, education, and other social sectors than at any time in its history. Moreover, government budgets are much larger than 10 or 20 years ago, both for the various line ministries working out of Ulaanbaatar and among the many local governments based in the provinces. Indeed, Mongolia's total national budget increased nearly ten times in nominal terms between 2001 and 2012.

Looking ahead, there is little doubt that good governance remains a fundamental challenge for Mongolia. More than any other issue, the country's performance here will likely determine the extent to which ordinary Mongolians benefit from the "mining boom" or are left behind because of it. Good governance will also go a long way toward determining the level of social stability in Mongolia as well as the strength and durability of its democracy. The cautionary experiences of mineral-rich countries elsewhere provide grounds for pause, especially as concerns about income inequality and corruption mount. Mongolia will face extreme challenges in the years ahead, and the jury is still out as to whether or not it will ultimately succeed.

* * * * * * *

The nature of the development partnership between the United States and Mongolia has changed over the years, even as the Mongolian economy has changed. While involved to some extent in policy dialogue during the late 1990s and early 2000s, when Mongolia continued its shift from a command-based to a market-based economy, USAID supported a series of "hands-on" initiatives intended to demonstrate in more concrete ways the "nuts-and-bolts" aspects of business development.

During the late 1990s, for example, USAID emerged as one of the original international donors to design a truly rural-based initiative. Similarly, in the early 2000s USAID became among the first to promote business-related activities in Mongolia's rapidly growing *ger* districts. The urban-based program was known as the Ger Initiative and implemented by CHF, formerly called the Cooperative Housing Foundation. Both rural and urban programs involved USAID directly in promoting credit and business services to low-income Mongolians, whether in the countryside or the crowded, rapidly growing *ger* districts surrounding Mongolia's three largest cities, Ulaanbaatar, Darkhan, and Erdenet.

As one of the first donor initiatives aimed at rural Mongolia, the Gobi Initiative had an immediate impact, assisting herder groups and promoting entrepreneurship in both *aimag* capitals and *soum* centers, first in the southern Gobi region and then in many other parts of Mongolia. In addition, the Gobi Initiative pioneered a wide variety of media products focused specifically on rural Mongolia, including the magazine *Rural Business News* and the radio serial *Herder from the Future*. At the same time, it made a conscious effort to expand the quality of information transmitted to the countryside, in part through initiatives such as *MarketWatch* and *WeatherWatch*, eventually reaching audiences estimated at more than half a million.

Looking back, the legacy of both the Gobi and Ger Initiatives lives on in the many hundreds, even thousands, of businesses that have been founded or assisted across Mongolia. Working with a variety of local partners, the Ger Initiative alone helped form more than 180 business associations, create more than 1,200 new businesses, and generate more than $50 million in sales. In addition, it led to the establishment of the well-known local consultancy group, Development Solutions, an organization that continues to promote small business development across Mongolia.

* * * * * * *

In retrospect, USAID work on both policy and practical "hands-on" project development came together in a most dramatic fashion in the early 2000s in the all-important banking sector. Indeed, the impact there has been far-reaching, among other things resulting in the founding of XacBank, the revitalization of Khaan Bank, and the privatization of the Trade and Development Bank. Today, all three banks rank among the top four in Mongolia. Both XacBank and Khaan Bank have now been privately owned and operated for many years—but it is highly unlikely that either bank would even exist without significant prior USAID involvement at a time when both were weak and struggling institutions.

The story of Khaan Bank—previously known as the Agricultural Bank of Mongolia—represents an especially notable success. As a government-owned entity, the Agricultural Bank had a long and undistinguished history of failure, having been bankrupted twice despite receiving large infusions of donor assistance as well as government funds paid for by Mongolia's taxpayers. Typically, the bank was at its weakest following elections, having engaged in a globally familiar pattern of "directed lending" focused more on winning votes than on achieving any kind of sustainable development.

For government policy makers struggling to keep it afloat, the Agricultural Bank increasingly seemed like the proverbial "problem child" or, perhaps more accurately, "the problem from hell." By the late 1990s, it had been so badly mismanaged and made so many problematic loans that one international consultant hired by a leading international financial institution could see no way forward. Asserting in his final report that the Agricultural Bank was "irreparably damaged," he added that no amount of remedial intervention could possibly save it, and the only realistic remaining course of action was to "shut it down."

Despite this dire prognosis, USAID did something that few donor agencies would ever dare to do—it assumed a lead role on the governing board and direct, "hands-on" responsibility for the entire range of operations of an essentially bankrupt bank. This decision was made at the Mongolian government's request in August 2000, a request driven primarily by the government's reliance on the Agricultural Bank to deliver both credit and salaries to teachers, doctors, nurses, and other government workers in the countryside.

During the innovative 30-month restructuring and remedial program that followed, the small USAID-funded management team headed by Peter Morrow, an experienced banker from Arizona, entirely "rebranded" the Agricultural Bank, relaunching it as Khaan Bank, a name that resonated strongly with Mongolia's impressive history going back to the days of Genghis Khan. As part of the rebranding, the management team—consisting largely, though not exclusively, of Mongolians—also introduced a new logo, new computer technology, new loan products, and in many cases new staff selected on the basis of merit rather than political connections.

Within six months, Khaan Bank had been returned to profitability. Some of the measures that made this possible seem obvious only in retrospect. "Before we took over, pensioners would go to their local branch to wait for payments in cash," recalls Morrow. "The government typically ran weeks or months behind on payments and rarely had enough money to pay everyone. So pensioners would jostle, sometimes even fight, for a favorite spot in line to make sure they got paid."

To remedy the problem, Khaan Bank introduced a direct deposit system, allowing pensioners to simply access their savings accounts rather than having to wait in line to collect a cash payment. At the same time, Khaan Bank extended a loan to the Pension Authority in Ulaanbaatar to ensure that the government could always cover its pension obligations on time. As a result of this creative effort, nearly half of Mongolian pensioners opened accounts at Khaan Bank.

Bank restructuring programs are often associated with ruthless staff reductions and a wholesale closing of branch offices deemed unproductive. However, under USAID stewardship the number of Khaan Bank branch offices actually increased from 269 to more than 350, and the number of bank staff doubled from 800 to more than 1,600. At the same time, the bank extended more than 400,000 loans and provided financial services to more than 500,000 households. In addition, staff salaries increased and training opportunities expanded dramatically. By 2012, the number of Khaan Bank branches had crossed the 500 mark, and the number of employees exceeded 5,000, virtually all of them Mongolian.

The success of Khaan Bank during those years had other positive consequences. For example, Khaan Bank pioneered new approaches to corporate arts support and philanthropy, as it set about acquiring one of the country's best private collections of contemporary Mongolian art. Perhaps most important of all, Khaan Bank was transformed in a short time from being a net drain on government resources to becoming one of the largest taxpayers in Mongolia.

As the once-bankrupt bank became solvent, the dramatic turnaround was featured in several international publications, including the *Far Eastern Economic Review* and *Asian Wall Street Journal*. The success of Khaan Bank provided me a convenient excuse, as USAID country director, to visit every one of Mongolia's 21 provinces. These visits provided useful opportunities to meet with not only bank managers but also local officials and clients from across the country. In cases where small district towns did not have a bank, officials and local entrepreneurs invariably pleaded that a branch of Khaan Bank be opened as soon as possible in order to stimulate more economic activity.

What was noticeable even then was that loans from Khaan Bank were already beginning to make an important difference, among other things making possible the wave of new purchases—solar panels, satellite dishes, portable televisions, and motorcycles—quickly being adapted for countryside use. Between 2002 and 2009, the number of herder families who owned solar panels increased from 15 percent to 75 percent. Years later, whenever I see the familiar green and white Khaan Bank signs in some of the most isolated and remote settlements in Mongolia, I recall those difficult early days when the very future of Khaan Bank hung in the balance and the consensus among many donors was to simply "shut it down."

Purchased by a Mongolian-Japanese consortium for $6.85 million in March 2003, Khaan Bank has emerged in recent years as a unique and perhaps unprecedented "success story" for Mongolia, winning numerous international banking awards along the way. Moreover, the new owners immediately hired the USAID-funded management team, using their own funds to ensure the bank's continued success rather than having to rely on Government of Mongolia subsidies or US taxpayer support.

During the two and a half years that USAID managed Khaan Bank, it allocated approximately $3 million to fund the management team headed by Pete Morrow and mobilized by its American consultant, DAI. Already the largest bank in Mongolia in terms of number of branches, by 2007 Khaan Bank also ranked as the largest in terms of assets, loans, deposits, and earnings. By 2011, Khaan Bank was worth as much as $100 million and had paid more than $40 million in taxes. Viewed from a broader perspective, the Khaan Bank story provides a tangible example of US-Mongolian cooperation in pursuit of sustainable development in Mongolia.

USAID's contribution to the establishment of XacBank is equally inspiring and has had a similarly dramatic impact on Mongolia's initially modest but now rapidly growing financial landscape. Established only in 2002, XacBank was formed following the merger of two donor-funded nonbank micro finance institutions, one supported by USAID and the other funded by the UN Development Program (UNDP). Early on, the new bank proved successful, attracting additional investment and gaining notable experience in how to design, implement, and sustain effective micro credit programs in a large, sparsely populated country.

Much of the credit for XacBank's early success goes to Stephen Vance, at that time country director for Mercy Corps in Mongolia and one of the main architects of the USAID-funded (and later USDA-supported) Gobi Initiative. Tragically, several years later Vance was killed in Peshawar, having assumed responsibility for a USAID-funded rural development program in Pakistan's tribal areas bordering Afghanistan.

Despite its modest beginning, XacBank has grown rapidly and in 2012 was regarded as one of the largest, best managed, and most successful private banks in Mongolia. It still maintains a commitment to micro finance while pioneering a range of other financial products, including mortgages and leasing. Having subsequently received additional support and investment from Triados, the European Bank for Reconstruction and Development (EBRD), the International Finance Corporation (IFC), and other international financial institutions, it has played an important part in strengthening Mongolia's banking and financial sector.

Mongolia still faces big challenges in banking and across the financial sector. However, at a micro level, Khaan Bank and XacBank represent success stories of the highest order. Both institutions also pioneered the use of Internet banking and ATM machines in Mongolia. Despite the vast distances that would seem to make banking in Mongolia risky, if not unprofitable, proportionately more Mongolians now maintain deposit accounts than is the case in any number of other countries spread across Asia, including Russia, India, China, Vietnam, Indonesia, and Kazakhstan.

* * * * * * *

While entailing fewer financial resources, USAID programs concerning governance and democracy have helped further strengthen the US-Mongolian development partnership. For example, during the early 2000s, the USAID-funded judicial reform project implemented by the National Center for State Courts (NCSC) trained hundreds of judges and helped computerize almost every courtroom in the country. Reflecting high-level US interest in judicial reform, the NCSC program in Mongolia was officially launched by US Supreme Court Justice Sandra Day O'Connor during a visit she made in September 2000 to speak in Ulaanbaatar at a conference on legal issues.

USAID programs in Mongolia included several initiatives dealing with the environment. For example, during the late 1990s and continuing into the early 2000s, USAID funded a co-operative arrangement with the US Department of Interior, leading to study tours of American national parks and the placement of former National Park Service staff from Alaska in Hovsgol National Park for several years. This initiative also supplied communication equipment to park staff and helped build a new information center at Hovsgol.

Starting in the mid-2000s, USAID environmental funding was targeted on the eastern part of the country, including support for the Wildlife Conservation Society's work with local communities to help preserve habitat and protect the gazelle. Wildlife Conservation Society research focuses on surveys, animal genetics, foot and mouth disease, and wildlife management and conservation. Given that gazelle migrations know no boundaries, efforts have also been made to engage with international NGOs, as well as local governments in neighboring Russia and China, to help ensure the survival of one of the greatest wildlife spectacles in the world—the movement of tens and even hundreds of thousands of gazelle each year across Mongolia's Eastern Steppes.

* * * * * * *

While USAID in recent years has emphasized sustainable development, from time to time USAID's Office of US Foreign Disaster Assistance (OFDA) has joined with other international donors to respond to dire and even unprecedented emergencies. The first such USAID disaster assistance was offered long before the formal January 1987 opening of diplomatic relations between the United States and Mongolia.

During the mid-1960s, some two decades earlier, the United States offered emergency assistance through the Mongolian Red Cross in the aftermath of flooding on the Tuul River that killed dozens and caused enormous amounts of damage to property. Though not publicly acknowledged at the time, very probably this offer of emergency relief represents the first official effort on the part of the United States to provide humanitarian assistance to Mongolia.

In subsequent years, the United States has on several occasions provided emergency assistance to Mongolia through USAID/OFDA, most notably during and after harsh winter *dzuds* in 2000–01 (nearly $730,000) and again in 2010 (approximately $300,000). At other times, USAID worked with Mongolia's National Emergency Management Agency (NEMA) and other local institutions on disaster preparedness and risk reduction, including programs to improve medical facility preparedness and the capacity to deal with disasters and to increase knowledge of earthquake risks among schoolteachers and students. Between 1993 and 2011, USAID/OFDA provided nearly $1.4 million to Mongolia to help in these and other efforts.

****

In January 2004, the United States established a new development assistance mechanism, the Millennium Challenge Corporation (MCC). From the outset the MCC provided grant funding aimed at addressing economic growth through poverty reduction, with an explicit focus on countries demonstrating a sustained commitment to good governance, economic freedom, and investments in people. MCC also placed a strong emphasis on diligent cost-benefit analyses, measurable goals, and effective monitoring and evaluation.

Based on these MCC criteria, Mongolia was among the first countries eligible for an MCC Compact program. During 2005–07, it initiated a process of large-scale public consultations across the country, preparing the ground for a consolidated set of funding proposals. On October 22, 2007, President Bush and President Enkhbayar signed the MCC Compact with Mongolia in the White House in Washington, D.C.—the first MCC Compact personally signed by a US president.

In keeping with MCC guidelines, the five-year, $285 million Compact between Mongolia and the United States aimed at reducing poverty and promoting sustainable economic growth. The new program, which more than doubled the amount of US grant assistance allocated to Mongolia, reflected a new approach to development partnership, one that placed the Government of Mongolia at the very center of the planning as well as the implementation process. The MCC Compact came into force in September 2008, formally launching a five-year time frame for project implementation, scheduled to end in September 2013.

MCC program implementation is the responsibility of the Millennium Challenge Account–Mongolia (MCA), a stand-alone entity based in Ulaanbaatar and specifically established by the MCC Compact. The MCA is headed by a senior Mongolian, who is responsible for a staff numbering well over 100, almost all of them Mongolian. Specific MCA programs have a number of priorities, including infrastructure ($86 million), health ($39 million), property rights ($27 million), vocational education ($47 million), and energy and environment ($47 million), all areas deemed high priority by the Mongolian government. The fact that MCC funds are not "tied" in any way also means that the technical assistance, training, and other support the MCA provides has come from many sources, including not only the United States but also Germany, Finland, Denmark, South Korea, China, and elsewhere. When accusations of corruption or misuse of funds have arisen from time to time, they have been investigated and, where appropriate, dealt with.

One of the most enduring MCA legacies is likely to be the 176.4 kilometer road through the Gobi region that connects Choir with Sainshand on the southern route to China. When officially opened in late 2013, the Choir-Sainshand highway will complete the last missing link of paved, all-weather road connecting Europe with East Asia via Mongolia.

In fact, the Choir-Sainshand road project was a "second-choice" initiative, the initial plan having been to use MCC resources designated for infrastructure to invest in railways jointly owned by Russia and Mongolia. However, it proved impossible to carry out required audits and undertake other needed preliminary work, and funds were therefore reallocated to build a road through the Gobi desert. Because the proposed MCC-funded railway initiative later had to be abandoned, some in the media ascribed geopolitical machinations to the decision, suggesting that the project failed because Russia was opposed to it.

Whatever the truth of that claim, the Choir-Sainshand road proposal quickly emerged as a viable alternative that also made an important contribution toward strengthening Mongolia's limited transportation infrastructure.

Health-related MCA-sponsored programs in Mongolia have emphasized noncommunicable diseases. This focus is directly linked to Mongolia's current health and mortality profile, which indicates that too many Mongolians die far too early from more traditional "Western" diseases such as cancer, diabetes, heart ailments, and road accidents.

The MCA program includes a strong public health and educational outreach component that extends to all 21 of Mongolia's provinces and involves dozens of health-related NGOs, both local and national. It also provides vehicles, health equipment, and other material to government health centers across Mongolia. Finally, it is improving public health education in Mongolia, in part through a partnership that has been developed between the Mongolian University for Health Sciences in Ulaanbaatar and George Washington University in Washington, D.C.

Property rights form the foundation for any market-based economy. Under a related initiative, the MCA is working with the Government of Mongolia to improve the efficiency and effectiveness of the state urban property registry process. Ultimately, as many as 75,000 households in Ulaanbaatar and eight regional urban centers, including Erdenet and Darkhan, should benefit as they are given the opportunity to register their properties in various *ger* districts and assume legal ownership. Already, the project has upgraded the geospatial infrastructure needed for accurate land mapping, in part by providing global positioning systems equipment to the various regional land offices.

In addition, the MCA is working to introduce a new system of leasing pasture land in rural areas immediately adjacent to Ulaanbaatar, Darkhan, Erdenet, Kharkhorin, and Choibalsan. In each case, these areas, which provide meat, milk, and other important agricultural products for Mongolia's urban population, face immense and growing pressure as urban Mongolia continues to expand into the countryside. Herders in these areas will also benefit from new wells, fodder, seed, fences, and winter shelter as part of a broader effort to improve livestock management and reduce the degradation of Mongolia's vulnerable pasturelands.

As Mongolia's economy expands dramatically during the coming years, there will be opportunities for many young Mongolians to find employment—but only if they have the right technical skills in place to meet expected demand. The mining and construction sectors in particular will create many thousands of new jobs that can and should be filled by Mongolians.

Based on MCA programs, the Great Hural passed new legislation that promotes reforms in the structure and content of vocational education and training in Mongolia. Measures are also underway to strengthen existing vocational training institutions, provide additional equipment, improve classroom space, and strengthen ties between private firms and public vocational training institutions. As with health programs, the vocational program initiative is national in scope and should benefit every part of the country.

Finally, the MCA directly addressed environmental concerns that rank among the most serious issues facing Ulaanbaatar. Vehicles, dust, industrial pollution, and smoke from the *ger* districts—all contribute to an untenable air pollution situation, especially in winter months when a thick, black pall of smoke often envelops Mongolia's capital city. As a result, Ulaanbaatar now bears the dubious distinction of being the second most polluted city in the world.

The MCA response embraced a series of activities aimed at introducing new energy-efficient heating products, including cooking stoves and new insulation products to mitigate pollution and improve air quality. The MCA program focused entirely on the *ger* districts of Ulaanbaatar, home to approximately 180,000 households and some 500,000 people. By 2012, well over one-third of these households had purchased new and more efficient MCA stoves, lowering pollution while also lowering fuel costs by as much as 30 percent. Beyond the nearly 70,000 fuel-efficient stoves distributed in the single winter season of 2011–12, a further 18,000 *ger* insulation sets had been distributed, contributing to a reduction in both pollution and fuel costs. In addition, pilot MCA projects have demonstrated the positive effects of more fuel-efficient housing as well as more efficient boilers.

Another component of the MCA energy effort involved development of Mongolia's first commercial wind farm at Salkhit ("Windy Mountain") near Ulaanbaatar. The wind farm, featuring GE turbines, is designed to reach a capacity of 50 megawatts, providing an important new source of energy for Ulaanbaatar while also demonstrating the viability of wind power in Mongolia. It is exactly the kind of investment that USAID hoped for when it funded Mongolia's first "wind atlas" a decade earlier, based on the expectation that wind, solar, and other forms of renewable power do indeed have a positive future in Mongolia.

As the MCC program enters its final phase of implementation in Mongolia, there are high hopes that all these projects—selected, designed, shaped, and implemented under Mongolian supervision and often involving Mongolian contractors or subcontractors—will make a major contribution toward strengthening economic growth, reducing poverty, and improving the quality of life in Mongolia. At the same time, continued concerns over corruption could undermine Mongolia's efforts to effect a second compact, to begin in fall 2013 or beyond.

****

Finally, other parts of the United States government, such as the US Department of Agriculture (USDA) and the Department of the Treasury, have made notable contributions toward strengthening the US-Mongolian development partnership. Historically, the USDA program in Mongolia has largely consisted of American wheat and other agricultural commodities that are donated to Mongolia. Proceeds from the sale of these commodities are in turn allocated for a variety of development purposes.

Since the 1990s, "monetized" programs from USDA valued at more than $80 million have been helpful in funding a wide range of activities, including rural road construction, research on yak production, and small business development. At one point, monetized proceeds from US wheat sales in Mongolia were used to help establish Mongolia's first Internet site—magic.net. USDA funds have also been used to support the ongoing work of various American NGOs based in Mongolia, including both CHF and Mercy Corps.

In 2009, the launch of an active US Department of the Treasury program marked the start of yet another chapter in US-Mongolian development relations, this one organized within the context of the global financial crisis of 2007–08. As a first response, USAID provided a $10 million cash transfer in 2009 to the Government of Mongolia as part of a much larger international effort that included several other donors to meet immediate foreign exchange shortfalls.

At the same time, the Department of the Treasury used additional USAID funds to provide both long-term and short-term technical advisors, first to the Mongolian Central Bank and then to its Ministry of Finance. The intent from the beginning was to strengthen Mongolia's fragile and highly stressed financial sector, in part by applying "lessons learned" and "best practices" from other countries that had successfully weathered similar crises in the past. Finally, in spring 2010, USAID provided initial funding to enable the Treasury Department to launch a technical assistance project at the General Directorate of Tax (GDT), aimed at improving capacity in the audit of specialized industries, including Mongolia's growing mining sector.

Chapter 5

Building Commercial Ties

"Long ago American merchants had settled in that area."

Early black and white photographs from the beginning of the 1900s give some indication of a United States commercial presence in Mongolia going back more than a century. Two of the more well-known American trading houses at the time were "Andersen and Meyer" and the "Mongolian Trading Company," the latter based in the Inner Mongolian town of Kalgan but with branch offices in both Urga and the western town of Uliastai.

Indeed, one photo dating to 1918 shows a Mr. Holman, one of the more prominent American business executives of the period, posing outside a large *ger* decorated with wolf skins. He is standing near a sign that describes his trading business as an "American Joint Stock Company." American silver dollars were legal currency throughout Mongolia at the time, along with Chinese silver ingots, and bank notes and coins from Russia and elsewhere.

Documents from the Mongolian National Archives provide tantalizing glimpses into other aspects of the early commercial relationship. For example, one document dated October 9, 1922, includes a request from an American citizen named Franche Menin to dig for gold. Another document, dated January 25, 1923, describes a possible conference on trade issues sponsored by British and American companies. Yet another document from the National Archives, this one dated to 1922, includes a query from the Mongolian Ministry of Foreign Affairs requesting information about the potential purchase of cotton from the United States to make military uniforms.

These early commercial ties played out in other ways as well. In the Mongolia Society's published version of Frans Larson's short, hand-written "memoir"—written late in life, long after his better-known first memoir, *Duke of Mongolia* (1930)––G. Ganbold's introduction includes a fascinating and almost certainly apocryphal anecdote about "American *Denj*" (meaning "American hill" or "American terrace"), the place in Ulaanbaatar where many American businesses first established themselves during the early 1900s. "There remains from these years a name for a specific area in present-day Ulaanbaatar, in the eastern district—where I used to roam as a schoolboy—a place called 'American Hill'," Gandbold recalls, linking his childhood with the earlier business exploits of Larson and other entrepreneurs from the United States and elsewhere who sought business opportunities in Mongolia. Ganbold writes:

> Though it was not the official name, it was widely used. It was explained to me by an old man that long ago American merchants had settled in that area. . . . [A]n American trader had asked for a piece of land as big as a cowhide to erect his warehouse. Since he asked for only a cowhide-sized plot of land, city authorities did not bother to refuse, because it seemed so small. When the permission was given, the American merchant sliced up his cowhide to make a huge rope, demarcating his newly given estate, which turned into a pretty big area.

It is not entirely certain if Larson—who had ties to both Sweden and the United States—ever set up shop in American *Denj*. However, he was certainly one of the most intriguing and colorful business characters of that period, standing out among his fellow expatriates for his love and knowledge of Mongolia. "Big business can be done successfully in Mongolia," Larson claimed in *Duke of Mongolia*, "but the trader must be possessed of the tact of the diplomat and be of a character which makes him akin to the people of the plateau and able to understand the conditions there." According to Larson, "a thorough knowledge of the language and a wide Mongolian friendship are the first requisites of success."

Larson had high praise for the early Russian tea traders in Mongolia who, he wrote, did "extremely well," noting, "They treated the people who freighted for them thoughtfully and generously." He also recalled prospectors from both Russia and France visiting the northern regions of Mongolia in search of gold. While the engineers involved in subsequent projects largely came from Europe and the United States, most of the labor was Chinese because "digging great quantities of gold out of the earth did not appeal to the Mongol as a profitable way in which to spend his days." Larson's account highlights some of the concerns that still mark discussion about doing business in Mongolia today, including references to a lack of infrastructure and an uncertain and sometimes capricious business environment. Larson's own business interests centered largely on wool, fur, and horses, and he claimed to have "exported more than two hundred thousand horses and a proportionate quantity of wool and furs" during the 35 years he worked in Mongolia.

Larson was one of a small number of foreign business executives and traders of that period to leave a written record behind. However, a few scattered details from other sources working out of American *Denj* are also available. For example, one American visitor in 1910 estimated that Mongolia exported 160,000 pounds of wool to the United States each year. By 1919, another American company was believed to be exporting $3 million in wool to the United States, while an estimate from 1921 speaks of "one million marmot skins" from Mongolia exported to the United States via Kalgan and Tianjin.

Another American company—one of a number with substantial ties to Mongolia at the time—apparently maintained seven "purchasing points" across "Outer Mongolia" from which to procure mutton. As for Anderson and Meyer, its early activity included the purchase and export of 3,000 to 4,000 race horses to China annually. Even in those years, rumors of Mongolian mineral wealth abounded, leading to much speculation and some modest investment in Mongolia's gold and silver mining sector.

Pioneering merchants from the United States also played a role in the introduction of the automobile to Mongolia. As noted earlier, the first motor-powered vehicle ever to be driven in Mongolia almost certainly was a Model-T Ford imported by an American entrepreneur. During the World War I years (1914–18), American companies such as Meyer and Larson pioneered the first "taxi" routes between Urga in "Outer Mongolia" and Kalgan in "Inner Mongolia," introducing vehicles manufactured by both Dodge and Ford to traverse the formidable Gobi on a regular basis.

These tough vehicles carried passengers as well as cargo, facilitating transport in the years before a railway line was constructed. According to former ambassador Joseph Lake, "In 1990 Mongolians still reminisced about the quality of the Dodge trucks from this period." Eventually, firms from other nations entered the transport sector, offering tough competition to the Americans on the Gobi route that they had pioneered. However, by the mid-1920s it was political pressure rather than competition that caused the American commercial presence to at first diminish and then disappear entirely. By the late 1920s, commercial ties between the United States and Mongolia had been abandoned altogether, seemingly never to revive.

* * * * * * *

The official opening of diplomatic ties between the United States and Mongolia in January 1987 did not immediately result in a revival of economic activity on any large scale. According to the Department of State Economic Fact Sheet prepared in January 1991 for President Ochirbat's visit to the United States, in 1989 the United States exported products worth $30,000 to Mongolia and imported products valued at $1.6 million; and the following year, US exports to Mongolia were placed at $50,000, and US imports from Mongolia were estimated at $1.9 million. It is very likely that many of these imports to the United States were via Boris Shlomm's Amicale, an American company that started operations in Mongolia during the Soviet era and largely specialized in the cashmere industry.

As these figures suggest, what little trade existed between the two countries was extremely modest, consisting almost entirely of cashmere wool and various animal by-products, virtually all of it in the form of Mongolian exports to the United States. At the time, Mongolia imported almost no American products. According to Ambassador Lake, the first American trade mission to Mongolia was sponsored by the Hong Kong American Chamber of Commerce and took place in the fall of 1990. Various investment and other economic agreements signed during the 1990s brought with them the expectation of a growing commercial relationship, including the Investment Incentive Agreement (September 29, 1990), the Agreement on Trade Relations (January 23, 1991), and the Reciprocal Investment Agreement (October 6, 1994). Realistically, such documents reflected aspirations more than reality in regard to any immediate growth in actual trade and investment figures. However, they did at least affirm the sense that, at some future point, a more vibrant commercial partnership might eventually be possible.

During the 1990s and into the early 2000s, a number of American business "pioneers" began to visit Mongolia in search of adventure as well as economic opportunity. They included Ed Nef, who launched Santis as one of Mongolia's first English-language schools; Ed Story and Wallace Mays, who made early investments in Mongolia's mineral sector; Pete Morrow, who for nearly a decade served as CEO of Khaan Bank; Jalsa Urubshurow, who launched Nomadic Expeditions as a high-end tourism venture; Lee Cashell, who focused on real estate; and John Karlsen, who was the catalyst for a dramatic expansion of Caterpillar in Mongolia. Two long-established Ulaanbaatar restaurants—Millie's and Sacher's Café—also have American connections, one founded by Millie Skoda, the other by Brigitte Cummings. Both women are American citizens, though in one case with ties to Ethiopia and in the other with links to Germany. For these and other early American business venturers, involvement in Mongolia sometimes became almost a "lifetime" commitment.

Given the importance of aid relations at the time, a number of the early members of the US business community working in Mongolia initially arrived to implement projects funded not only by USAID but also by various multilateral donors such as the World Bank, the Asian Development Bank, and various UN agencies. Still, whether measured in services or the value of trade, business ties between Mongolia and the United States remained at a low level, perhaps in part due to the geographic distance separating the two countries.

* * * * * * *

By the late 1990s, quotas on foreign apparel exports to the United States briefly appeared to offer an avenue for a more robust trade relationship. The industry involved only modest start-up costs, encouraging investors from China and elsewhere to set up garment factories in Ulaanbaatar and Darkhan with the sole aim of exporting clothing to the United States.

The volume of these clothing exports increased markedly during the late 1990s and into the new millennium. However, a garment industry based solely on quotas proved unsustainable, especially after China's accession to the World Trade Organization in 2001. By 2004, Mongolian exports to the United States—consisting mostly of apparel—peaked at nearly $240 million. After that, they fell dramatically, barely exceeding $50 million by 2008 and falling still further in the following years. In retrospect, the rapid rise—and almost as rapid plummet—in garment exports from Mongolia to the United States can be viewed as a "false dawn" that initially seemed promising but ultimately proved unsustainable. At some level, it also offered an early lesson in international competitiveness and the formidable challenges facing Mongolia in the international marketplace, most notably the high transportation costs and long production lead-times imposed by Mongolia's remote location. Since the collapse of the apparel industry, Mongolia has gravitated toward a more specialized and, one hopes, more sustainable export garment "niche" largely involving higher value and higher-quality items, primarily related to cashmere and cashmere products, with yak and camel wool occasionally also entering into the mix. Indeed, despite pricing challenges, Mongolian cashmere producers such as Gobi, Buyan, and Altai are finding international markets not only in the United States but also in Korea, Japan, Europe, and elsewhere.

* * * * * * *

Despite a very slow start throughout the 1990s and into the 2000s, exports from the United States to Mongolia began in 2010 to show every sign of increasing dramatically in the years ahead. The path to growth should also be much more sustainable, especially if Mongolia's mining industry "takes off" as expected and is accompanied by a steady expansion in the number and types of downstream support industries. Mongolia's efforts to develop new industrial approaches that add value to its mineral products should also offer significant opportunities to American businesses, especially those that provide the services, machinery, and other material that Mongolia will need as it builds up its own industrial sector. Looking back, the arrival of Wagner-Asia in 1996 as an all-American company with strong ties to Colorado may be regarded as one of the turning-points in US-Mongolian commercial relations, carrying with it not only the promise of high profile American name brands such as Caterpillar and Ford but also a long-term commitment to "growing" a business based on an overwhelmingly Mongolian workforce. In fact, Wagner-Asia's growth over the last decade largely mirrors that of Mongolia's. As an early entrant into the Mongolian marketplace that has stayed the course and emphasized its long-term commitment, it has reaped benefits based on its understanding of the broader Mongolian social and economic terrain.

Wagner-Asia's commitment to training Mongolians in technical skills has won considerable praise, including its recruitment of young Mongolians skilled in math and science, even from remote provincial towns across the country. Once identified, these young Mongolian high school graduates are then trained through an impressive series of high-quality hands-on courses, turning them into skilled mechanics who will be in high demand during the coming years.

By 2010, Wagner-Asia was maintaining offices in Ulaanbaatar, Darkhan, and Khan Bogd in the south Gobi. While it has seen huge growth in its mining equipment division involving Caterpillar and other brands, it is also involved in Mongolia's potentially large agricultural sector. More than 98 percent of the Wagner-Asia labor force, which grew from approximately 300 staff in 2009 to nearly 1,000 by 2012, is Mongolian.

Other US based companies are increasing their presence in Mongolia. In the mining sector, some of the more familiar names include Fluor, which is involved in the copper and gold mine at Oya Tolgoi, and Peabody, which is competing to play a major role in the coal mine at Tavan Tolgoi. In reality, the growth in direct US investment in Mongolia through 2012 remained at somewhat disappointing levels, paling in comparison with the growth in exports. So far, it is much smaller than similar investments emanating from China and various "third neighbors" such as Australia and Canada. This could change in the years ahead, especially if American firms such as Peabody are selected to take on major mineral projects.

While both actual and potential US investment in Mongolia is most closely associated with the minerals sector, American business executives have displayed interest in other areas. For example, Eagle Television was launched as a media venture with missionary connections in the early 1990s at a time when Mongolia's independent media were just developing. Although the US partners sold their interest in Eagle to Mongolian investors in 2011, their involvement over several years introduced Western-style approaches to media coverage and set new standards in television reportage and production, which other stations in Mongolia have sought to emulate with some success.

More recently, Bloomberg television launched business-oriented programming in Mongolia in July 2012, opening its studio in a spacious new office building overlooking Sukhbaatar Square and offering at least four hours of locally produced Mongolian-language television programming each day. Here again, the quality standards and production values of Bloomberg are likely to have a "ripple" effect, eventually leading to improvement in the economic and business coverage offered by other Mongolian media outlets.

American business executives, managers, and consultants have also been highly visible in other sectors, including the financial sector, where they have assumed key management roles in banks such as Khaan Bank and XacBank. In the hospitality and tourist industry Americans have made management contributions on various occasions to the Ramada, Genghis Khan, Bayangol, Terelj, and other hotels and invested in tourist companies such as Nomadic Expeditions. As the Mongolian economy continues to expand, one can expect opportunities for still more US involvement in Mongolia's financial, legal, and service sectors in the years ahead.

* * * * * * *

The opening of an official General Electric (GE) office in Ulaanbaatar in May 2011 represented yet another landmark in the continued growth of US-Mongolian business ties over a relatively short period. Viewing Mongolia as a growing market with considerable potential, GE focused in its initial stages on potential markets related to both energy and medical equipment.

One of GE's first major contracts in Mongolia involved providing turbines for the 50 megawatt MCC-supported wind farm built by the Mongolian company Newcom at Salkhit mountain, not far from Ulaanbaatar. GE is also competing for major contracts in Mongolia's transportation and power sectors, including the provision of train engines for Mongolian Railways and the supply of turbines for a public-private sector partnership aimed at building Ulaanbaatar Five, Mongolia's first really significant new investment in power generation since the Soviet era.

US exports to Mongolia increased markedly following Mongolia's recovery from the effects of the international financial crisis during 2007–08. For comparative purposes, it is worth recalling that total US exports to Mongolia in 2001 measured a paltry $12.1 million before rising to $66.3 million in 2002. After that, they remained "stuck" within the $20 to $30 million range for the next several years, from 2003 through 2007. The 2008 figure, rising to $57.2 million, seemed to offer some optimism about the future—a hope that was dashed in 2009 when

US exports to Mongolia fell to around $40 million, as the entire world faced a serious economic downturn.

Responding to the challenges posed by the international financial crisis, President Obama early in his administration committed the United States to doubling its exports worldwide in the five years between 2009 and 2013. For Mongolia, the timing was propitious, given that Mongolia was already well on its way to economic recovery while also experiencing the first fruits of what could be an extended mining boom. In fact, US exports to Mongolia grew at an extraordinarily rapid pace from 2009 to 2010, increasing by 180 percent to more than $110 million. That pattern of dramatic growth continued into the following year. During the first half of 2011, US exports to Mongolia exceeded $160 million and, by the end of the year had exceeded $313 million. Put another way, in the case of Mongolia, President Obama's five-year export target was easily met—in a single year.

* * * * * * *

The US embassy in Ulaanbaatar actively promoted stronger business relations between the United States and Mongolia as early as 1991, starting with the arrival of Alaina Teplitz as the first embassy economics officer. Leah Camper—spouse of early Wagner-Asia representative Rodney Camper—served as the first commercial assistant within the US embassy starting in 1998.

Also in 1998, Brian DaRin—a former Peace Corps volunteer—wrote the embassy's first business guide. In more recent years, the annual embassy-issued "Investment Guide to Mongolia," posted on the embassy's Internet site, provides an objective, candid, and sometimes hard-hitting perspective on both the positive and negative features of the Mongolian investment climate. While offering "sober optimism" about future business prospects in Mongolia for those considering investments, it also provides useful cautionary notes on the very real difficulties confronting the international business community, including lack of confidence in the sanctity of contracts, fears about expropriation, and concerns about growing corruption.

Leah Camper was followed as commercial specialist by two former Peace Corps volunteers, first Alison Croft and then Michael Richmond, who arrived in 2000 and remained in place the next 12 years and beyond. By and large, the embassy commercial office has been staffed by locally hired Americans who have years of prior experience in Mongolia and can offer important advice and "ground-truthing" about Mongolia's business climate to prospective investors when they first arrive in Ulaanbaatar.

Commercial section activity out of the US embassy in Ulaanbaatar deals with networking and distributing relevant information. One especially effective program involves linking the Mongolian business community with US companies through attendance at trade shows, conferences, and other events. Important sectors such as mining, construction, and agriculture have figured prominently in the list of shows that Mongolian business executives now routinely attend across the United States.

The US Department of Commerce plays an active role in facilitating these trips. In recent years, approximately 500 Mongolians annually have regularly attended US-based trade shows, providing useful exposure to new products and strengthening US-Mongolian business ties still further. In addition, the Commerce Department has been organizing annual US-Mongolia business forums, which facilitate commercial opportunities between American and Mongolian businesses.

From time to time, the US embassy has encouraged the growth of organizations designed to promote broader commercial concerns. For example, the embassy supported the establishment of the American Business Group (ABG) in 1991, which later formed the basis for the American-Mongolian Business Council (AMBC). The AMBC, in turn, expanded to include a Canadian dimension, resulting in the North American-Mongolian Business Council (NAMBC). For many years, NAMBC has been headed by businessman Steve Saunders, who has been visiting Mongolia since 1994 and takes the lead in organizing annual NAMBC conferences in both Mongolia and North America. In 2011, a Mongolian-American Chamber of Commerce headed by former IRI country representative Jackson Cox was also established.

Steve Saunders, along with Pete Morrow, throughout his years at Khaan Bank, has promoted business ties in other ways, such as helping to establish the Business Council of Mongolia (BCM) in fall 2007, an organization with a reach that extends well beyond companies from Canada and the United States. The BCM has grown dramatically, its membership rising from 35 in 2007 to more than 240 Mongolian and international members by the fall of 2012. It is headed by Jim Dwyer, an American businessman who first arrived in Mongolia in May 2001 as part of a USAID-funded initiative to support the privatization of the Trade and Development Bank and Khaan Bank.

Outside work, Jim Dwyer played a lead role in founding the Giant Steppes of Jazz NGO, which sponsors an annual jazz festival each fall. That such a contribution would come from within the American business community seems especially appropriate, given that some Mongolians believe it was an American sales representative working for the Ford Motor Company who first introduced jazz to Mongolia during the early 1900s. According to the legend, which is still repeated in Ulaanbaatar to this day, the Ford representative also happened to play jazz piano—and sometimes entertained the Bogd Khan at his summer and winter parties when he visited Mongolia from China.

The growing Mongolian community in the United States plays a useful role in further strengthening business ties between the two countries. Having been exposed to American food products and various consumer goods, some entrepreneurial Mongolians simply load a container with goods purchased at discount stores in the United States such as Sam's Club and ship them to Ulaanbaatar for wholesale or retail sale. Such initiative helps expose Mongolians to American products, which can expand markets still further. The impact of this practice can be seen in a variety of shops in Ulaanbaatar bearing the names of American cities and towns, such as Oakland, Seattle, and New Orleans—and, on occasion, a "Made in America" label painted red, white, and blue and displaying the Stars and Stripes.

* * * * * * *

As Mongolia's economic relations with the United States and other countries become increasingly based on commercial rather than development ties, opportunities for trade and investment between the United States and Mongolia should continue to expand. US government organizations such as the Overseas Private Investment Corporation (OPIC), Ex-Im Bank, and the Trade and Development Agency (TDA) can be expected to play an even more important role in facilitating that commercial relationship.

During President Elbegdorj's visit to the United States in June 2011, he was accompanied by a large group of Mongolian business executives, most of whom met American counterparts in a conference sponsored by TDA in Washington, D.C. Beginning in 2002, TDA has financed several agreements with Mongolia related to aviation management and safety, including separate agreements with both Eznis and MIAT Mongolian Airlines.

More significantly, during the same visit President Elbegdorj, along with US Secretary of Commerce Gary Locke, witnessed at Blair House the signing of an agreement between MIAT and Boeing to move Mongolia's national airline toward becoming an all-Boeing fleet. As a first step, the agreement provided for the purchase of three Boeing jets—two 737s and one 767—valued at $245 million. A Memorandum of Understanding (MOU) on trade and economic cooperation between the US Department of Commerce and the Mongolia Ministry of Foreign Affairs and Trade was also signed during this visit. At some point there could be direct flights between Ulaanbaatar and the west coast of America, although that day has not yet arrived.

Senior American officials involved in business relations and economic affairs are increasingly making their way to Mongolia. Assistant Secretary for Trade Promotion and Director General of the Foreign Commercial Service Suresh Kumar, for example, visited Ulaanbaatar in October 2011, meeting with government officials, journalists, and members of the American business community. Then in May 2012 Fred Hochberg, chairman of the Ex-Im Bank, paid a visit. During his stay, he signed a Memorandum of Understanding with Batjargal Bazarsuren, chairman of the Development Bank of Mongolia, aimed at promoting trade and investment between the two countries.

Despite these encouraging developments, there is a widespread belief in both the American business community and among those who follow Mongolia from a more political perspective that economic and commercial ties between the two countries are still not nearly as robust as they ought to be. Since 1990, the bigger story of Mongolia's trade and investment ties with the rest of the world has been the significant growth in interaction between Mongolia and China, largely at the expense of Russia, which once dominated every aspect of Mongolia's economy. By 2012, almost all of Mongolia's exports were bought by China—and the largest share of its imports came from China. At the same time, Russia retained its market share of exports to Mongolia only in major commodities such as wheat and petroleum. While the United States in recent years has typically ranked second in terms of its share of exports to Mongolia, it lags far behind China; and in a typical year its performance only slightly exceeds that of other "third neighbors" such as South Korea and Japan.

Mongolian officials have on occasion expressed frustration about their inability to move forward with a Free Trade Agreement with the United States. For their part, American officials have voiced similar concern about a noticeable lack of progress on a transparency agreement aimed at ensuring a level playing field for commercial activity, whether involving local or foreign companies. From an American perspective, a transparency agreement would send a strong message about Mongolia's willingness to promote a more open, consistent, and transparent business environment, one that aspires to world standards while also taking an aggressive stance against corruption.

As Mongolia's economy continues its dramatic expansion, one hopes that the opportunities for US-Mongolian business and commercial ties will experience more rapid growth in the years ahead. Investments in the mining sector clearly attract special attention and garner most of the international headlines. Yet, over the long term, interest in other sectors such as livestock, agriculture, tourism, and real estate is also likely to increase. If Mongolia manages to successfully weather the challenges of a resource-rich economy, diversify its sources of economic growth, and ensure that the benefits of mining are widely shared, investment should expand in any number of other areas. Mongolia's infrastructure requirements alone are massive, and US-based businesses, along with those from other countries, are likely to take a strong interest in participating in this expansion.

Chapter 6
Promoting Security

"Bridging the land of the blue sky with the land of the midnight sun"

While diplomatic ties between Mongolia and the United States formally commenced in January 1987, it would be nearly a decade before those relationships included a strong security dimension. The foundational document for such an engagement was signed in Ulaanbaatar on June 26, 1996. It established a framework for what has become an important and mutually beneficial partnership covering a broad range of areas, including military exchanges and annual joint exercises.

Following the agreement, the Marshall Center in Garmisch, Germany, provided several Russian-speaking American officers to serve in the US embassy as defense liaison officers for terms of four to six months. Colonel Mike Byrnes, serving as nonresident military attaché, helped arrange the first of a series of US military flights, bringing relief supplies at a time when Mongolia faced severe economic difficulties. At one point during the mid-1990s, winter relief supplies were air-dropped into Mongolia's far western province of Bayan Olgii.

Colonel Larry Wortzel, at that time the army attaché in Beijing, became the first US military attaché accredited to Mongolia in 1995, even before the 1996 security assistance agreement between Mongolia and the United States was signed. Major John Baker, one of the early short-term officers from Garmisch, later returned to Mongolia on a full-time basis starting in 1999, becoming the first full-time, resident US military attaché assigned to Ulaanbaatar and making the US embassy one of only three foreign embassies in Ulaanbaatar—along with Russia and China—to have a military attaché in Mongolia.

Major Baker in turn was followed by six other attachés with the rank of lieutenant colonel—Tom Wilhelm, Mark Gillette, Antonio Chow, Matthew Schwab, David Tatman, and Jonathan Lau—each of whom, together with their Mongolian and American staff, played an important part in expanding and deepening the ongoing and productive engagement on security issues now in place between the United States and Mongolia.

Efforts to work together to promote security in Northeast Asia and beyond have taken many forms. Partly, it involves continued dialogue on perceptions aimed at advancing peace and stability in a strategic corner of the world. Mongolia borders Russia and China and is situated in close proximity to Japan and the two Koreas. It is also close to Kazakhstan and shares historic and even cultural ties with the whole of Central Asia, stretching from Kazakhstan to Afghanistan, including Kyrgyzstan, a country that traces its ancient history back to Lake Kyrgyz in Mongolia's western Uvs province.

From a US perspective, Mongolia's experience and viewpoint have much to offer to neighbors in Central and Northeast Asia, including lessons learned from both its "decision for democracy" in the early 1990s and its continued shift from a Soviet-style command economy to one shaped in significant part by market forces.

Beyond the ongoing strategic dialogue, the United States has joined with numerous other countries to promote a professional working relationship with the Mongolian military. This interaction helped Mongolia in its rapid emergence as a contributor to UN peacekeeping operations abroad; provided support for Mongolian deployments as part of coalition efforts in both Iraq and Afghanistan; and assisted in the development of a world-class training center at Five Hills, 30 miles west of Ulaanbaatar, which deals primarily with international peacekeeping. Other aspects of the US-Mongolian partnership on the security front include continued efforts to better secure Mongolia's borders and ongoing work with both civilian and military institutions to strengthen emergency preparedness should Mongolia ever face severe earthquakes or other natural disasters.

On May 27, 2012, I joined ambassadors from several other countries—including Germany, France, the United Kingdom, Canada, Japan, Laos, Vietnam, North Korea, South Korea, Turkey, and China, among others—in marking UN Peacekeeping Day on Sukhbaatar Square in central Ulaanbaatar. Resident military attachés from Russia, China, and the United States participated in the commemoration events, along with hundreds of soldiers and their families, as well as ordinary Mongolian citizens interested in this display of their country's military prowess.

As it happened, the occasion also marked the tenth anniversary of Mongolian participation in UN peacekeeping missions overseas. During those first ten years, Mongolian troops participated in 14 such missions, providing opportunities for Mongolia to contribute to global security in places as far afield as Kosovo, Sierra Leone, Darfur, and South Sudan. As part of the ceremony, President Elbegdorj bestowed newly minted "Peace in Africa" and "Peace in Afghanistan" medals on some of the many hundreds of Mongolian soldiers, both men and women, who participated in international peacekeeping in far-flung corners of the world over the past decade.

* * * * * * *

The rapid transformation of Mongolia's military from a Soviet-style static army to a deployable, well-trained, mobile international peacekeeping force is a notable achievement. It was only in 2002 that Mongolia's Great Hural first passed legislation authorizing Mongolian soldiers to serve abroad. Two years later, Major General Gur Ragchaa was posted as the first military advisor to the Mongolian Permanent Mission to the United Nations. His assignment later played an important part in Mongolia's increasing contribution to UN peacekeeping assignments in Africa and beyond.

In August 2002, the first two Mongolian officers served as observers attached to the UN peacekeeping force in the Democratic Republic of Congo. Later that year, Mongolia also sent observers to another UN peacekeeping mission, this time in Western Sahara. Since then, Mongolian soldiers have taken on a variety of international assignments, serving with coalition forces in Iraq and Afghanistan and contributing to UN peacekeeping efforts in Sierra Leone, Liberia, Kosovo, Chad, Sudan, and elsewhere.

Although a number of countries have assisted Mongolia in its efforts to forge a new type of military able to deploy as part of UN peacekeeping and other operations overseas, US contributions played an especially useful role in terms of both training and equipment. As part of this continuing security partnership, the United States has made important contributions to the growth and development of the Five Hills Training Center, refurbishing buildings, providing equipment, facilitating training programs, and assisting in the emergence of Five Hills as the only peacekeeping training center of its kind in all of Northeast Asia. By the end of 2011, US financial contributions toward strengthening Five Hills had exceeded $5.7 million.

Mongolia is already well on its way toward achieving its long-term objective of developing and putting into place a world-class, 3,000-person peacekeeping force. This is an ambitious but achievable goal for an army numbering only 12,000. While consisting mainly of highly mobile infantry, this new Mongolian peacekeeping brigade will ultimately also include military police, engineers, and medical personnel.

Mongolia first deployed troops to Iraq in August 2003. Over time, it provided more than 900 military personnel, who served in ten consecutive rotations with the Polish-led Multinational Division that included soldiers from 21 other countries.

The most dramatic event in Mongolia's Iraq deployment occurred in the second rotation, when a suicide bomber driving a truck laden with explosives attempted to drive into the Polish camp at Hilla. Charged with protecting the perimeter, the Mongolian security force moved into action immediately with deadly accuracy, killing the terrorist driving the truck before he had time to explode his truck inside the camp. Following this attack, the two soldiers most directly involved—Sergeant Azzaya and Sergeant Samuu-Yondon—received combat medals and were recognized as "Mongolian heroes," both in Poland and in Mongolia.

A few months later, in October 2003, the first Mongolian soldiers deployed in Afghanistan, their numbers expanding significantly as military operations in Iraq began to wind down. By the end of 2010, approximately 200 Mongolian soldiers were serving in Afghanistan, some staffing guard towers at Camp Eggers in Kabul, others training soldiers of the Afghan national army near Kabul in artillery systems and helicopter maintenance. Still others worked with Belgian soldiers at Kabul airport and with German troops in Faizabad in northern Afghanistan. Early in 2011, President Elbegdorj announced at the NATO summit conference in Madrid that Mongolia intended to double its Afghan deployment to 400, proportionately one of the most significant contributions made by any country to the Afghan campaign.

****

In March 2011, I joined embassy defense attaché Lt. Colonel Lau to spend several days with the Mongolian soldiers serving in Afghanistan. It was a moving and inspiring encounter, starting with the initial parade and martial arts demonstration that concluded with pinning the International Security Assistance Force (ISAF) medals, with blue and white ribbons, on each member of the contingent as they neared the end of their rotation.

We carried with us Mongolian-language newspapers and magazines, messages from Mongolian school children, brick tea and *taiga* tea from Lake Hovsgol—and fresh *aaruul* (cheese) from the Mongolian countryside. Our admiration and respect for the Mongolian troops serving far from home only increased when we visited their living quarters and saw snapshots of loved ones back in Mongolia and pictures of horses, *gers,* and the never-ending steppe posted on the walls of their recreation center, built within the shadow of the snow-covered Hindu Kush.

Meeting for a bowl of *airag* in the ceremonial *ger* that Mongolian soldiers had constructed at Camp Eggers, I was reminded that it was nearly 800 years ago that Mongolian soldiers had last watered their horses in the Kabul River. Although Genghis Khan's favorite grandson was killed while fighting at Bamiyan, he considered Afghanistan as his "favorite" part of the world after Mongolia. Given the weather, climate, historic landscapes, and wide open spaces, it was not hard to see why.

Even today, Afghanistan's Hazara minority who live in the central highlands of the country view themselves as the descendants of Genghis Khan's soldiers, a feeling reinforced by the fact that "Hazara" in Farsi (as well as in Urdu and several other South and Central Asian languages) means thousand, the size of a standard detachment within the army of Genghis Khan. Not surprisingly, Mongolian soldiers deployed in Afghanistan felt a special affinity with the country's Hazara population from the very beginning. In fact, as a result of the Afghan deployment, the Mongolian government now sponsors several scholarships for Hazara students from Afghanistan to study in Ulaanbaatar, and at least one private Mongolian university offers additional scholarships to Hazara students.

At one point during my visit to Kabul in March 2011, I asked a Mongolian soldier about his encounters with the Afghan Hazara population during his deployment in Afghanistan. "Oh yes, we have met several times," he replied. "One of them even asked of us—'Why did you ever leave us behind?'"

In April 2012, the Mongolian Ministry of Foreign Affairs and Trade (MFAT) made its own contribution toward stabilizing Afghanistan, providing a two-week training course for young Afghan diplomats to learn from the Mongolian experience. Twelve Afghan diplomats participated in a series of field trips and classroom exercises, each aimed at introducing them to Mongolia and its economy, society, and role in the world.

Among other things, the MFAT training course introduced the Afghan diplomats to Mongolia's "third neighbor" foreign policy. This included both the challenges and opportunities associated with being surrounded by larger and more powerful neighbors, along with an interest in seeking "balance," in part by also reaching out to other countries as well as the UN, regional groups, and other multilateral organizations. There were also discussions about the problems faced by landlocked countries and the challenges experienced in managing mineral-rich economies. According to one of the Afghan diplomats who attended the training course in Ulaanbaatar, "We came to understand that there is much more to Mongolia than what we were taught in our history books back in Afghanistan."

Beyond Afghanistan, Mongolian soldiers have also distinguished themselves in other UN and NATO peacekeeping assignments over the last decade, winning growing recognition and respect for Mongolia's professional military. For example, about 70 Mongolian military personnel served in the NATO Kosovo Force (KFOR), working largely with the French battalion. Hundreds of Mongolian soldiers have also been assigned to Freetown, the Sierra Leone capital, to provide security for the UN Special Court for Sierra Leone.

Over the past decade, Mongolian military observers have gained valuable additional experience in UN peacekeeping operations through their work in the Congo, Western Sahara, Sudan, and Ethiopia. In addition, Mongolian units have served in larger numbers as UN peacekeepers in Chad. More recently, in December 2010, several dozen Mongolian medical personnel, many of them women, were deployed in nearby Darfur, establishing a military hospital using medical equipment donated by the US Air Force valued at more than $4.2

million. In early 2012, the first members of a Mongolian contingent that eventually numbered 850 began deploying under the UN flag in the world's newest country, South Sudan.

Perhaps the most important element in Mongolia's emergence as a peacekeeping nation is the international character of its global engagement. In this regard, US assistance for training and in providing nonlethal equipment has helped complement assistance offered by other nations, including Mongolia's immediate neighbors. For example, Russia provided most of the heavy equipment used by the Mongolian contingent in Chad, including armored troop carriers. Similarly, China assisted Mongolia by funding construction of a "rest and recuperation" center in the hills outside Ulaanbaatar, set aside for use by Mongolian soldiers and their families after the rigors of their peacekeeping assignments abroad.

At a multilateral level, Mongolia's contributions have not gone unnoticed, garnering for both Mongolia and its military a well-deserved reputation for dedication, commitment, and professionalism. As a result of this service overseas, it is not uncommon to meet Mongolian soldiers or border guards in even remote parts of the country who are well traveled, having been deployed in various peacekeeping operations in Africa, the Middle East and elsewhere.

****

American and Mongolian participation in two annual military exercises have helped deepen their security partnership still further. One, Khaan Quest, focused on international peacekeeping and typically occurs in the summer. The other, Gobi Wolf, scheduled in the spring, involves domestic disaster preparedness. Less regularly scheduled exercises have occasionally been centered on Mongolia.

The first joint Khaan Quest exercise was held in Mongolia in May 2003 as a bilateral exercise between the US Marine Corps and the Mongolian armed forces. Subsequent Khaan Quest exercises have been held on an annual basis. Beginning in 2006, Khaan Quest became a multinational exercise, involving not only US and Mongolian soldiers but also those of many other countries, including South Korea, Japan, Singapore, India, Fiji, Cambodia, Thailand, Tonga, Nepal, and others. The Khaan Quest exercise held at Five Hills outside Ulaanbaatar in August 2011, involved many hundreds of soldiers representing 19 different countries.

Often Khaan Quest exercises have also benefitted local civilian populations, especially regarding various outreach programs. Over the years these programs have brought medical care to thousands of Mongolian patients in remote, underserved locations. In 2010, for example, US doctors, nurses, and medical staff teamed up with their Mongolian military counterparts to provide optometry, dentistry, neurology, obstetrics-gynecology, internal medicine, pediatrics, surgery, and pharmacy services to the population of several districts in Mongolia's Omnogobi province. Additionally, veterinary support was provided to local herders. Similarly, engineering cooperation has brought tangible benefits to local communities, as illustrated by the 2010 Khaan Quest exercises, when US soldiers and their Mongolian counterparts built a public bathhouse in one of the *ger* districts of Ulaanbaatar.

Outreach programs were also arranged as part of the Khaan Quest exercise in August 2011, resulting in more than 5,000 medical consultations in *ger* districts in the western part of Ulaanbaatar near the airport. At the same time, military engineers from the United States, India, and Mongolia worked together to enlarge and improve a community health unit in the same area.

That same summer, the US Air Force's annual "Pacific Angel" humanitarian exercise dealt specifically with Mongolia. An international effort involving soldiers from several countries, the medical outreach this time centered on Henti province, east of Ulaanbaatar and regarded as the historical home of Genghis Khan. As in Khaan Quest, military doctors associated with Pacific Angel treated thousands of patients, while a contingent of soldiers worked to refurbish a rural health center.

The annual Gobi Wolf exercise was based upon a 2008 workshop that reviewed the Mongolian government's responses to a simulated energy sector failure. Building on the success of this workshop, the first Gobi Wolf exercise was launched in March 2009 with support from the Hawaii-based Center for Excellence in Disaster Management and Humanitarian Assistance.

During the first year (2009), scenario planning revolved around a train derailment near Ulaanbaatar involving toxic chemicals. Subsequent Gobi Wolf exercises have addressed a possible mining disaster (2010) and a deadly earthquake (2011), potentially catastrophic events that require advance detailed planning to ensure an effective response, not only from the Mongolian military but also from civilian entities such as the National Emergency Management Agency (NEMA).

Other US programs provide training opportunities for growing numbers of Mongolian soldiers and civilians engaged in security issues. Some training is tactical or operational in nature, but much of it is strategic. Such training includes Mongolian participation in workshops, seminars, and academic programs sponsored by major American military institutions such as the Army War College, the Army and Air Force Command and General Staff College, the National Defense Intelligence College, the National Defense University, the Industrial College of the Armed Forces, and the Naval Post Graduate School. Many dozens of Mongolians have also participated in programs provided by the Asia-Pacific Center for Security Studies in Hawaii, and some have attended programs offered at the George C. Marshall Center in Germany.

Interaction with the Asia-Pacific Center for Security Studies is especially intensive. By 2011 the number of Mongolians participating in seminars, workshops, and other programs at the Center over the year passed the 150 mark. Participants represent many disciplines and areas of interest, including defense attachés and a large number of officials, both military and civilian, from the parliament, police, customs, internal troops, border forces, the Ministry of Defense, Mongolia's National Security Council, the Ministry of Foreign Affairs, the Ministry of Justice, the National Emergency Management Agency, the National Defense University, and the Institute of Strategic Studies.

Over the years, the alumni list from these institutions has reflected the active participation of a large number of distinguished Mongolians, including not only ministers, members of parliament, and ambassadors but also President Elbegdorj. Indeed, officials at the Center applaud Mongolia for the "diverse representation" of its participants—both men and women have attended, as well as officials representing the full spectrum of government, from parliament to many ministries.

The US-supported International Military Education and Training (IMET) program plays a significant part in strengthening Mongolian military capabilities and has provided much of the funding for training Mongolians on security-related topics. Funds are provided entirely on a grant basis. Specific programs deal with strengthening US-Mongolian military ties and promoting interoperability, partly by providing English language and other training. Between 1992 and 2011, the total IMET funding for Mongolia reached $13 million.

In addition, US-Mongolian co-operation is advanced through the Foreign Military Financing (FMF) program. Under this initiative, the United States funds on a grant basis a range of nonlethal military equipment requested by Mongolia, including uniforms, night vision equipment, and vehicles. Recently, Mongolia expressed interest in acquiring C-130 aircraft built in the United States in order to establish a "lift capacity," useful not only to deploy peacekeepers in the various international assignments but also to respond quickly, deal with potential natural disasters, and provide the prompt air response required in a country as large as Mongolia.

Finally, between 2002 and 2004 Mongolia received $2 million from the Enhanced International Peacekeeping Capabilities program. Not long afterwards, it became a partner in a similar US-funded Global Peace Operations Initiative (GPOI), receiving approximately $10 million in additional equipment. This support reflects appreciation for Mongolia's commendable record of service on numerous peacekeeping missions around the world as well as a desire to ensure that the military is well prepared for possible future deployments abroad.

* * * * * * *

While many Mongolian officers have studied in the United States in recent years, travel and training opportunities move in both directions. As a result, American military personnel have had the opportunity to visit, teach, train, and work in Mongolia. A unique program launched in 2005 and concluded in fall 2010 brought to Mongolia some 117 marines, almost all noncommissioned officers (NCOs), on a regular basis, temporarily embedding them for months at a time with Mongolian units training for overseas deployments.

The program gave Mongolian NCOs an opportunity to strengthen their professional skills and their ability to operate as leaders of small units in order to make them more effective as they prepare for their next overseas deployment. Marines who participated in this program also appreciated the chance to celebrate Mongolian festivals, hunt in the Mongolian countryside, and spend time with Mongolian families, strengthening people-to-people ties while also improving their military skills.

Starting in the early 2000s, American servicemen and women from the army, air force, and marines have also provided specialized subject-matter training in a number of areas, ranging from medical services to military police to combat engineering and explosive ordinance demolition.

One program even forged a co-operative relationship between various Mongolian army bands and their American counterparts. Perhaps the highlight so far of this particular program occurred in July 2010, when the US Marine Band based in Honolulu joined with their Mongolian counterparts for a well-received concert on Sukhbaatar Square that featured not only a marching band but also a joint jazz concert that concluded with Louis Armstrong's widely popular classic "What a Wonderful World."

****

The partnership launched in September 2003 between the Alaska National Guard and the Mongolian military represents one of the more interesting aspects of the security ties that have developed between the United States and Mongolia over the last decade. While the program strengthened military co-operation, it also forged useful partnerships in other areas, including health, disaster preparedness, and education. As the motto for this particular partnership suggests, the initiative plays an especially useful role in "bridging the land of the blue sky with the land of the midnight sun." And, as the program mission statement notes, the goal is to "link the Alaska National Guard with Mongolia for the purpose of fostering mutual interests and establishing relationships across all levels of society."

Part of an ongoing effort on the part of the United States is to link National Guard units of specific American states with more than 50 different countries, the "twinning" of the Alaska National Guard with Mongolian counterparts proved an inspired choice. Physically, Alaska and Mongolia are almost exactly the same size. They also share a number of other features, including a similar climate, low population density, and a mineral-rich economy. Going further back, linguists point to similarities between Mongolian and various native Alaskan languages that represent a lingering historical memory of the time when people from Central Asia crossed the then-existing "land bridge" linking the two continents and began to populate North America.

The military aspects of the Alaska National Guard partnership are perhaps best demonstrated in Iraq and Afghanistan, where American soldiers have shared danger with their Mongolian counterparts as comrades in arms in a war zone. For five years starting in April 2004, officers from Alaska "embedded" with Mongolian soldiers on duty in Iraq. This was followed by a similar arrangement in Afghanistan starting in September 2009. At Camp Eggers in Kabul, as in Iraq, Alaskan soldiers deploy with Mongolian soldiers, providing an important liaison and training function while also deepening understanding and respect between soldiers from the two countries.

Soldiers from the Alaska National Guard also participate in the annual Khaan Quest and Gobi Wolf exercises in Mongolia. In both instances, the participation of Alaskan military officers and civilian officials provides additional expertise while also enriching the security partnership.

As a result of the National Guard connection, Alaska twice hosted the US-Mongolia Defense Bilateral Consultation Council and contributed to civilian-focused activities such as annual medical readiness training exercises. Moreover, the connection helped the Mongolian military develop new approaches to family support, ensuring that the families of Mongolian soldiers deployed abroad also receive support back home.

Not surprisingly, the Alaska-Mongolia partnership through the Alaska National Guard quickly moved beyond military ties to strengthen relations in other areas. One outcome has been the development of a sister-city relationship between Fairbanks and Erdenet, which in turn has led to two full scholarships for students from Orkhon province to study mining engineering at the University of Alaska.

Former Ambassador Pamela Slutz, who helped launch the program, observed:

> One of the major advantages of the sister-city partnership was—and is—that it opens up educational opportunities for Mongolians: under Alaska state law, citizens of a town that has a formal sister-city partnership are entitled to study at the University of Alaska at reduced, in-state tuition rates. And Alaska has much to offer in terms of technical expertise and experience in mining under extreme climate and environmentally fragile conditions.

As a result of this educational policy, more than 20 Mongolian students from Erdenet City and Orkhon province are now receiving their higher education at the University of Alaska in either Fairbanks or Anchorage. Furthermore, there is a developing relationship between the University of Alaska at Fairbanks and the Mongolian University of Science and Technology. During the summer of 2011, those ties led to the establishment of a student exchange program in mining and engineering that will provide Mongolian students with still more opportunities to study in Alaska during the years ahead.

The partnership forged through the Alaska National Guard has also had other benefits. To highlight only a few, the Alaska-Mongolia partnership has so far provided opportunities for Mongolian health officials to visit Alaska, for Mongolian financial specialists to study the Alaska Permanent Fund as a potential investment mode, and for Mongolian law enforcement officials to meet with Alaska state troopers and Anchorage police officers. In recognition of the usefulness of the partnership, President Enkhbayar visited Alaska in October 2007.

Reflecting on partnership developed over the last several years, Craig Campbell, former lieutenant governor of Alaska and former adjutant general of the Alaska National Guard, notes that "only the National Guard" could be the catalyst for the broad range of military and civilian programs that have been launched in the last few years. According to General Campbell:

> It can't be done by the active duty military. It can't be done solely by the civilian community. The reason is, the National Guard brings significant civilian expertise. We're citizen-soldiers. The majority of us have civilian jobs. We have that experience and skills from doctors to engineers to carpenters. We're the only ones that have military and civilian combined in one package.

* * * * * * *

Finally, two notable US-sponsored programs assist in Mongolia's efforts to promote security by protecting its long borders, one in the area of communications and the other in monitoring the possible movement of nuclear materials across international frontiers.

The first program, known as the Border Forces Communications Project, was launched in 2000 and formally concluded exactly one decade later, in March 2010. During those ten years, the United States provided more than $9.2 million in grant funding to equip Mongolian border forces with Harris radios in Uvs province and elsewhere. The initiative, involving the provision of many small solar-powered systems, also provided direct contact between remote Mongolian border forces patrolling in the far northwest of the country and headquarters in Ulaanbaatar. In more recent years, the Harris radios have also ensured that Mongolian soldiers in both Iraq and Afghanistan could communicate directly with their headquarters back in Ulaanbaatar.

Without doubt, the opportunity to discuss this communications initiative and see it working in the field provided some of the most memorable moments of my ambassadorship in Mongolia. At different times, it was possible to meet with Mongolian border forces in Uvs in the far west and Dornod and Sukhbaatar in the far east. In each case, it was like going back in time, to when border patrols were conducted on horseback by small units provisioned, at best, on a monthly basis. Otherwise, soldiers were on their own, relying on their own herds of sheep for food. Wives and small children sometimes accompanied officers, living in nearby *gers* dozens of miles from the nearest hamlet. Under existing border protocols, the Mongolian border forces occasionally met and communicated with their Russian and Chinese counterparts on the other side of the frontier, sometimes to sort out issues involving local cattle rustlers. Such trips were a vivid reminder of the vastness of Mongolia as well as the challenges it faces in protecting its remote and far-flung frontiers.

The second program—part of the Second Line of Defense Radiation Portal Monitoring Program, sponsored by the US Department of Energy and involving a number of countries in Central Asia—was launched following the signing of a Memorandum of Understanding between the United States and Mongolia in Washington, D.C., on October 23, 2007.

From the beginning, the State Specialized Inspection Agency (now the General Agency for State Inspection) played a leading role on the Mongolian side. After its creation, the Nuclear Energy Agency (NEA) assumed policy authority, with the Inspection Agency a lead implementer along with the Mongolian border guards and Customs General Administration. From the start, the intent has been to strengthen Mongolia's efforts to deter, detect, and interdict illicit trafficking in nuclear and other radiological materials.

By 2011, the United States had provided some $20 million in equipment and training to Mongolia through the Department of Energy as part of this broader international effort to detect and monitor potential shipments of nuclear materials. Initially, portals were installed and became operational in November 2008 at several locations, including Ulaanbaatar, Sukhbaatar, Altanbulag, and Zamiin-Uud. Several additional sites have since come on line in northern and western Mongolia. Future portal installations are planned at additional sites on Mongolia's southern and eastern borders.

In these and other ways, the United States has supported Mongolia's own ongoing efforts to affirm its independence, preserve its sovereignty, and protect its international frontiers.

Chapter 7
Sustaining People-to-People Relationships

"If you care about what you do, you can overcome most barriers."

People-to-people relationships are the lifeblood of any bilateral partnership between countries, the foundation on which all other long-term engagements are built. Long before formal diplomatic relations were established, Americans and Mongolians were meeting together, sometimes in unlikely places. Photographs taken during the Roy Chapman Andrews expeditions to the Gobi during the 1920s attest to some of these early interactions. Even during the long decades of the Cold War, some Americans visited Mongolia as tourists or academics; and a few Mongolians visited the United States, primarily as dependents of Mongolian officials assigned as diplomats to the United Nations.

It was the opening of a formal diplomatic relationship between the United States and Mongolia in January 1987, however, that launched first a trickle and then a flood of interactions between Mongolians and Americans, both private and public. In fall 1989, McKinney Russell, one of the most senior public affairs diplomats in the US Foreign Service—and at that time head of the United States Information Agency office in Beijing—traveled by train to Ulaanbaatar to visit the very rudimentary American embassy then in place. "I did an analysis of the university, the cultural scene, the media," he later recalled. "It was great fun to be the first officer to go and talk to people to find out what the opportunities there would be for us when it did open up."

US public diplomacy in Mongolia has since increased exponentially, supplemented by numerous privately funded initiatives. Private relations include a growing number of visits by tourists and business executives as well as a variety of encounters that are academic, cultural, or religious in nature. By 2010, more than 10,000 American tourists were visiting Mongolia annually, while nearly as many Mongolians were taking the opportunity to travel to various parts of the United States.

The year-round American population living in Mongolia is estimated at approximately 1,500 and growing, primarily related to mining and other new business opportunities. Perhaps one-third are believed to be the children of Mongolian parents who were born in the United States and therefore have a claim to US citizenship.

Most Americans living in Mongolia reside in Ulaanbaatar, but some geologists, miners, and others live and work in the South Gobi and other areas of Mongolia rich in minerals. Also, several dozen American missionaries, NGO workers, and entrepreneurs have lived in Mongolia for many years, a few raising families in some of the more remote areas of Mongolia, including in unlikely smaller regional towns such as Choibalson in eastern Mongolia, Tsontsengel in Zavkhan, and Hatgal near Lake Hovsgol.

Private US citizens living and working in Mongolia have been involved in a range of activities in a variety of settings. For example, in recent years American volunteers have helped raise funds to provide new facilities for the Lotus Center, a well-known children's home located just east of Ulaanbaatar and run by Didi, a Buddhist nun from Australia. Other private US citizens have addressed social issues, taught English, managed hotels, launched bakeries, opened restaurants and coffee shops, addressed environmental concerns, restored historical monuments, promoted wrestling exchanges, and played in Mongolia's professional basketball league.

American NGOs often facilitate private encounters with Mongolia. These include World Vision, which funds community development programs across Mongolia; Habitat for Humanity, which has built or improved housing for more than 1,500 Mongolian families since 2000; Experiment in International Living, which introduces American high school students to life with Mongolian herder families on the steppe; and the Snow Leopard Trust, which works to conserve and protect snow leopards in western Mongolia.

* * * * * * *

The number of Mongolians living, working, or studying in the United States on a long-term basis far exceeds the number of Americans resident in Mongolia. Since the establishment of diplomatic relations in 1987, the US embassy in Ulaanbaatar has issued more than 70,000 visas of all types to Mongolians for business, tourism, study, and migration purposes. At this point, the number of visas issued annually by the embassy now exceeds 10,000 and is growing rapidly.

By now, the number of Mongolians living in the United States almost certainly exceeds 20,000, placing the United States as the second most popular destination for expatriate Mongolian citizens living abroad; only South Korea with a resident Mongolian population of more than 30,000 ranks higher. This figure does not include other ethnic Mongols and their descendants who arrived in the United States prior to 1990, including Kalmyks and Buryats from Russia and other Mongols who trace their origins to Inner Mongolia and now live in the United States. If these additional communities are taken into account, the total number of ethnic Mongolians living in the United States is even larger.

Alicia Campi who heads the Mongolia Society, has noted:

> The first Mongolian Khalkha to immigrate to the United States was a well-known lama, the Dilowa Gegen Khutukhtu. He had been a government official and headed a monastery in Mongolia but fled the country during the anti-religious purges of the 1930s, when some lamas left Mongolia for India.

Subsequently, the Dilowa traveled to the United States in 1949 to work with Owen Lattimore in Baltimore. Smaller numbers of other Mongolians also later migrated to the United States by way of Tibet and India.

As with every migrant population, it takes time for a Mongolian community to take root and firmly establish itself. Many Mongolians originally came to the United States as students or tourists, and their average age remains quite young. While migration from Mongolia to the United States increased substantially after 1990, significant numbers are "visa overstays" who have not yet legalized their status and will not necessarily set down long-term roots in America. According to the Mongolian academic Tsendiin Baatar, "a distinctive cultural heritage is being maintained despite Mongolian participation in many of the national institutions of the American host culture." As economic opportunities in Mongolia increase, more Mongolian citizens working abroad are beginning to return to their homeland to contribute to their country's development.

The Mongolian-American community includes some Christians, while others affirm and strengthen their ties to Buddhism during their stay abroad. For example, Mongolians play a significant role in the Tibetan Mongolian Buddhist Center in Bloomington, Indiana, which in turn enjoys a close relationship with both the Dalai Lama and Ulaanbaatar's Gandan monastery. The large Bloomington complex is situated on 108 acres and includes a monastery and cultural building along with stupas and retreat cottages. Smaller temples with a strong Mongolian influence are located in New Jersey, New York, Pennsylvania, Illinois, Colorado, and California.

In a pattern typical of many migrant communities in the United States, Mongolians themselves organize a variety of community structures, not all of them religiously based. The list of such organizations includes the Washington Area Mongolian Community Association and the Mongolian School of the National Capital Area, Inc. Similar efforts are underway in Denver, Oakland, Chicago, and elsewhere.

Over time, these and other institutions almost certainly will add to the depth and breadth of people-to-people relationships among Mongolians and Americans alike. When visiting the Mongolian Community Center in Oakland, California, in October 2010, I was warmly welcomed by Mongolians who were simultaneously establishing one foot in the United States while also remaining linked to their home country. One teenage girl showed me a copy of the contemporary romance novel *Coral Bracelet* that she had translated from Mongolian into English with encouragement from one of her high school teachers. Other students related their efforts to introduce Mongolia to their American classmates.

During that same visit to the Mongolian Community Center in Oakland, I was told about the annual *Naadam* festival in the Bay Area, an annual midsummer celebration of Mongolian culture and athletic prowess that attracts several thousand participants each year. In fact, *Naadam* celebrations have become regular attractions in a number of different states. For example, during the summer of 2012, *Naadam* festivals were organized in parks and other venues across the United States, including Altadena, California; Arlington, Virginia; Bloomington, Indiana; and Chicago, New York City, San Francisco, Seattle, and Tampa.

Almost always, encounters with Mongolians living in the United States provide insights into both the struggles and opportunities faced by a new immigrant community seeking to establish itself. For example, on one visit to Washington, D.C., in late fall 2009, I had the privilege of meeting a Mongolian single mother and her son in Arlington, Virginia. They had been awarded entry to the United States under the annual "visa lottery" program and were already well on their way to becoming US citizens. The son, enrolled in a local high school, had already scored a touchdown for his junior varsity football team and tried out for his school wrestling team, hoping eventually to win a scholarship to wrestle in college.

He would be following a path that other Mongolians studying in the United States on athletic scholarships have pioneered. For example, one member of the Mongolian national soccer team, formerly a member of the soccer club Ulaanbaatar United, finished the 2010–11 season as the leading goal scorer for his college team in Texas, Central Methodist University. Mongolian collegiate wrestlers in the United States have won a number of awards, including one young man studying at the Citadel in South Carolina, who earned a "conference wrestler of the year" award in 2011, and another studying at St. John's in Minnesota, who was declared "NCAA Division III college wrestler of the year," also in 2011. Indeed, it is possible to imagine the day when an American citizen of Mongolian origin competes in the Olympics under the American flag, one of any number of "success stories" that reflect America's truly multiethnic society.

****

Perhaps nothing promotes long-term people-to-people ties between countries more than educational exchanges and scholarships. Since USAID sponsored the first four Mongolian students to study in the United States in 1990, the educational component of the US-Mongolian relationship has dramatically expanded. The number of Mongolians studying in the United States increases every year. Many hundreds of Mongolians now find their way to American colleges and universities annually, some using personal resources, others as recipients of private scholarships, and still others under government-sponsored scholarship programs.

Since its inception in 1993, the Fulbright program has been regarded as among the most prestigious of all US government scholarships available to Mongolians. Originated by J. William Fulbright, a prominent U.S. senator with a longstanding interest in foreign affairs, the program is managed by the Public Affairs section of the US embassy in Ulaanbaatar. Focused largely on graduate education by 2012 the Fulbright program had funded scholarships for more than 50 highly qualified Mongolians seeking MA and Ph.D. degrees in the United States.

In early 2011, the Mongolian government made its first direct financial contribution to the Fulbright program, providing an additional $300,000 to expand scholarship opportunities and allow a further ten Mongolians to earn MA degrees in the United States. As a result, 16 Mongolian graduate students had embarked on Fulbright scholarships for study in the United States in fall 2011—up from only three just two years earlier.

These Fulbrighters reflect a wide range of backgrounds and experiences. Fields covered include public health, international relations, biology, urban development, information technology, energy, psychology, law, public policy, education, and supply chain management. So far, the destinations of MA students under the Fulbright program include Brandeis, Georgia State, Harvard, Texas A&M, Illinois, Iowa, Nebraska, Montclair State, Lehigh, Stanford, Syracuse, the State University of New York, the University of California at Berkeley, and the John Marshall Law School in Chicago, among others.

Although the "core" Fulbright program provides scholarships for MA degree candidates, a variety of more specialized Fulbright initiatives support other study opportunities. For example, the International Fulbright Science and Technology Award is highly competitive, involving a worldwide selection process aimed at attracting to leading US institutions the "best and brightest" who are especially interested in math and science.

Another initiative, the Fulbright Foreign Language Teaching Assistant program, enables recent Mongolian graduates to spend a year in the United States helping to teach Mongolian to American students. Launched only in 2005, nine Mongolians enrolled in the program during its first six years of operation. Participating institutions in the United States so far include Michigan State, Pittsburgh, Indiana, and Western Washington universities.

While Fulbright scholarships largely involve graduate study, some programs specifically focus on undergraduates. In 2009, most notably, 12 such Mongolian students participated in an eight-week intensive English-language program in the United States that introduced them to American culture and society while also strengthening their English language skills. At the same time, other outstanding Mongolian undergraduates have spent either one or two semesters at US colleges and universities, experiencing US higher education firsthand through the Global Undergraduate Program.

The Fulbright program has also been expanded to provide opportunities for American students to study in Mongolia and for American professors to teach and conduct research in Mongolia. Launched in 2002, the program involved approximately 40 Americans during its first decade of operation. The Fulbright Specialist Program, for example, annually sends about five US scholars to study in Mongolia for two to six weeks. The American specialists partner with Mongolian counterparts and conduct workshops, give lectures, assist graduate students, or work with Mongolian scholars on joint research projects. Research funded under this initiative has included everything from anthropology and the arts to law and higher education. During 2012, one Fulbright researcher funded by MTV explored Mongolian music, looking specifically at the ways in which Mongolian musicians have responded to the dramatic changes underway in Mongolia in recent years.

The list of Mongolian Fulbright scholarship alumni continues to expand. Increasingly, returning Fulbrighters make their mark on a variety of Mongolian institutions, both private and public. One Fulbright alumnus heads the math and economics department at the National University of Mongolia; another served as human rights and social policy advisor for President Elbegdorj; and a third became a senior professor at the Mongolian School of Foreign Service.

In the private sector, Fulbrighters who have returned to Mongolia to work have included the chief financial officer for the TenGer Financial Group; the managing director and the head of the marketing department of Goyo Cashmere; the CEO of Max Hotels and Services; the director of the Genghis Movie Theater; and the sales and distribution director for MCS Coca Cola.

According to Fulbright returnee Ariuntsatsral Erdenebileg, who received a master's degree in Public Health at Georgia State University in 2009, her scholarship opened "a whole new door for my professional development." One of Mongolia's few female heart specialists, she works at the Third National Hospital and volunteers for the Children's Heart Project, a branch of the American NGO Samaritan's Purse. Under this program, in cooperation with American cardiologists working in hospitals across the United States and Canada, the latest surgical techniques have been used to save several hundred Mongolian children born with heart defects. "If you care about what you do," she says, "you can overcome most barriers."

Similarly, Gantuya Badamgarav, a Fulbrighter who studied at Williams College in Massachusetts, reports that she returned to Mongolia with a "deeper understanding about American culture and people," along with a strong desire to "make changes in our life, community, and country." She has pursued her objectives through her career in private business, her work in opening an art gallery, and her support for activities that benefit Mongolia's disabled community.

* * * * * * *

The Fulbright program is but one of several ways in which the US embassy works directly to provide study opportunities for Mongolians who wish to study in the United States. By the end of 2011, some 24 Mongolians had participated in the prestigious Hubert H. Humphrey Fellowship Program, named after the late US vice president and senator.

This program concentrates exclusively on early-and mid-career professionals. Mongolians awarded Humphrey fellowships have studied everything from natural resource management at Cornell University to educational administration at Vanderbilt University. Enkhtuya Oidov, one of many outstanding Humphrey alumni, studied at American University in Washington, D.C., and later became CEO for the Nature Conservancy in Mongolia. Subsequently, her son Badruun earned a scholarship to study at Stanford University, returning to Mongolia to head the Zorig Foundation.

Especially during the 1990s and early 2000s, USAID provided funding for Mongolian students to obtain MA degrees in the United States. Since 1996, some 23 Mongolians have received USAID scholarships for study in the United States at the master's degree level, returning to Mongolia to assume prominent positions both inside and outside government. The list of distinguished USAID scholarship winners is impressive and includes A. Munkhbat, senior vice president at Ivanhoe Mines; B. Enhhuyag, former deputy governor of the Mongol Bank; Z. Enkhbold, senior member of parliament, and Jargalsaikhan, bank executive, television host, and newspaper columnist.

USAID has also funded ten Eisenhower scholarships, the first having been awarded in 2001. The Eisenhower program, named after former US president Dwight Eisenhower, is short term in nature but involves an intensive, tailor-made study tour of the United States that provides access to the most senior levels of government and business.

Here, too, the alumni list is impressive, including among others Ts. Ariunna, executive director of the Arts Council of Mongolia; M. Ichinnorov, director of the Women's Leadership Foundation; D. Ganbat, director of the Political Education Academy; E. Sodontogos, personal assistant to the president; and S. Oyun, a member of parliament and former foreign minister. Three of the nine female parliamentarians elected to the Great Hural during the June 2012 elections were previous participants in the Eisenhower Fellowship program—S. Oyun, funded by USAID, and Batchimeg Migiddorj and Oyungerel Tsedevdamba, funded from private donations.

Finally, many dozens of Mongolians benefit from their participation in short-term programs such as the International Visitors Leadership Program (IVLP), which includes the Voluntary Visitors Program. Nominations for this program are managed out of the embassy's Public Affairs office, and project planning and implementation are managed by the Office of International Visitors in the State Department Bureau of Educational and Cultural Affairs. Topics cover a range of fields, from journalism to political processes to disability concerns. In every case, the intent is to provide opportunities for young Mongolian professionals to meet American counterparts and visit the United States, often for the first time.

The IVLP ranks among the earliest people-to-people programs launched by the US embassy in Mongolia. Approximately 200 Mongolians visited the United States under the auspices of the program from its establishment in 1989 through 2011. Prominent early visitors included former President N. Enkhbayar, who participated in a program on arts legislation in the United States in 1994, while serving as deputy minister of culture. Three years later, Erdenebulgan returned to Ulaanbaatar after his participation in the Visitor program to stage the Mongolian premiere of the American opera classic *Porgy and Bess*.

Often, a scholarship or study tour becomes an eye-opening experience, the effects of which continue throughout a lifetime. In some cases, the spouses of Mongolians who study in the United States return to their home country and do remarkable things. One Mongolian woman who accompanied her husband to his graduate study at the University of Wyoming became familiar with the 4-H program, an American initiative aimed at rural youth.

Impressed with the 4-H approach, she started a Mongolian 4-H chapter on her return. Subsequently, in 2011 she became the catalyst for a $222,000 State Department grant to promote an exchange between 4-H Club members in Mongolia and the western United States. As a result, some 34 high school students and their teachers from Wyoming, Oregon, Alaska, and elsewhere were able to visit Mongolia and stay with herder families in the countryside. The experience was repeated again in the summer of 2012, providing another opportunity for American high school students to interact with herder families and experience Mongolia for themselves.

In an effort to maintain contact and further strengthen ties among Mongolians who have studied or visited the United States, an alumni group called "Ambassadors for Development" was founded in 2007 at the initiative of several returned scholarship winners, including Enkh-Amgalan, Khongorzul, Batbold, Altantsetseg, and Ulziijargal. During 2011–12, *Ad Hoc* interviewer and journalist Jargalsaikhan served as president.

The organization can draw on a pool of approximately 750 returned alumni—a number that increases every year. Support is provided by returned Fulbrighter Uyanga Erdenebold, who serves as "alumni coordinator." Uyanga attended Louisiana State University and brought Mongolia's first guide dog back with her to Ulaanbaatar. Her experience in the United States has in turn been helpful in strengthening the embassy's understanding and information related to Mongolia's disabled community.

As members of Ambassadors for Development, returned alumni maintain contact with each other while also supporting various public service and outreach programs. Recent examples include two summer camps, both in 2009, organized by returned Fulbrighter Gantuya, which provided English language training to handicapped Mongolian children. According to returned alumnus Bolortungalaga, "One of the common wisdoms we learn and experience in the

United States is the value of social diversity and how this understanding leads to equal opportunities for everyone, including people with disabilities."

In addition to supporting the embassy's disability initiative, some returned alumni volunteer for Habitat for Humanity projects; others brief new scholarship winners as they prepare to depart Mongolia for their first visit to the United States. In January 2011, the US embassy worked with the alumni association to organize the first full-fledged alumni conference in Mongolia, an event that attracted more than 100 participants.

* * * * * * *

Official government-funded contributions can provide useful support, but the fact remains that most Mongolians studying in the United States do so on a private basis. According to the Institute of International Education's annual *Open Doors* report, which surveys international study by country, during 2009–10 there were more than 1,250 Mongolian students studying in the United States. Other estimates place the number of Mongolians currently studying in the United States at more than 2,500. Many of these students fund their education out of their own resources, while more than a few receive private scholarships from leading American colleges and universities. Others pioneer entirely new possibilities, such as B. Saruul, who in June 2012 became the first Mongolian student ever to enroll at the prestigious US Military Academy at West Point.

Recognizing the importance of personal initiative and private scholarships in obtaining higher education in the United States, the US embassy along with the Open Society Forum has for many years supported a growing network of Educational Advising and Resource Centers (EARCs), under the EducationUSA umbrella, not only in Ulaanbaatar but also in regional centers such as Darkhan, Dornod, Erdenet, Hovd, and, most recently, Sainshand. Each EARC provides free public access to educational information, including advice on scholarship programs in the United States and around the world. Some of those using EARC services have been offered scholarships to attend Harvard, Yale, Stanford, and other leading American universities.

Other US-funded programs provide a "window on America" in other ways. For example, following President George W. Bush's visit to Mongolia in November 2005, the embassy launched Mongolia's first English Access Micro Scholarship

Program. Focused on talented but disadvantaged 14-to-18-year-olds, many of whom live in *ger* districts, the Access program provides after-school instruction and intensive summer activities. While taking English language classes, participants also learn about and gain an appreciation for US culture and values. Some of the most satisfying moments during my own time in Mongolia involved encounters with the Access students and their understandably proud parents, who have sacrificed much simply for their children's opportunity to learn more.

From the launch of the Access program in 2006 through 2011, some 140 Mongolians living in Ulaanbaatar and another 60 Mongolians living in Hovd participated and improved their English skills, winning English Olympiad awards along the way. Some Access alumni have also begun to win scholarships to study abroad. Meanwhile, more than 80 children living in Mongolia's far western Bayan-Ulgi province have participated in a series of Access summer English language camps, the first of which was launched in 2007.

The development of "American Corners," first in Ulaanbaatar in 2004 and then in Hovd in 2008, has provided further opportunities for Mongolians to learn about the United States and for Mongolians and Americans to engage with each other on a person-to-person basis. Both centers are located in local public libraries, providing free access while serving as a useful center for information about any number of topics related to the United States.

Resources available at these two American Corners in Mongolia include Internet access as well as videos, books, and magazines. In addition, the American Corner in Ulaanbaatar provides weekly lectures in English on a wide range of topics. Typically, 40 or 50 Mongolians attend these lectures each week, providing opportunities for visiting Americans to meet with Mongolians, discuss any number of subjects and learn from each other.

* * * * * * *

Established by the US Congress in 2001, the US Ambassadors Fund for Cultural Preservation helps to preserve cultural sites, objects, collections, and forms of traditional expression. It plays an especially useful role in funding initiatives aimed at protecting Mongolian culture and presenting it to a wider audience. Individual US ambassadors at posts around the world solicit prospective projects before sending documents to Washington for a broader review in competition with proposals from dozens of other countries. Over the years, Mongolia has fared exceptionally well in this annual competition, garnering additional support for programs that strengthen cultural relations between the two countries.

From the launch of the program in 2001 through 2012, Mongolia received more than $300,000 under 12 different "small grants" provided by the Ambassadors Fund. The first, awarded in 2002, focused on preserving Mongolia's folk traditions and involved the Institute of Language and Literature at the Mongolian Academy of Sciences. Two years later, $30,000 was provided to support a team of scientists from Mongolia and the Smithsonian Institution to document 3,000-year-old carved stone plinths, known as Deer Stones, scattered around many unprotected sites throughout northern Mongolia.

In 2008, a further $39,000 was provided to help preserve and protect a series of Deer Stones in the remote Khanui Valley in the north central province of Arkhanghai. As former US Ambassador Mark Minton recalls, "Visiting these archeological digs in the field was one of the most memorable experiences I had during my three years in country."

A pioneering project of the Noyon Khutagt Danzanravjaa Museum near Sainshand, south of Ulaanbaatar received $28,000 from the Ambassadors Fund. The intent was to help preserve recently recovered manuscripts, books, religious items, personal possessions, and *tsam* dance costumes that once belonged to Buddhist monks in the area. The items were buried hastily during the 1930s at a time when monasteries across Mongolia faced destruction.

Remarkably, the location of this treasure was secretly passed on to a new generation; it was only in the 1990s that the location was finally revealed and some of the hidden chests were dug up. Danzanravjaa, often referred to simply as the "Lama of the Gobi," has himself become better known in recent years, both as a poet and as the orchestrator of lavish, colorful, and highly creative nineteenth-century dramas featuring *tsam* mask dances, a custom that is now being revived.

Several other Mongolian museums have also benefitted from these small grants, including the Zanabazar Museum ($18,000) and the Museum of Modern Art ($27,000) in Ulaanbaatar, both of which received support in 2010. The Zanabazar Museum grant was targeted on preserving and presenting objects from a seventeenth-century Tureg-era burial mound, while the grant to the Museum of Modern Art funded secure display cases that help protect paintings, sculptures, and other objects produced by Mongolian artists since the early part of the twentieth century.

In addition, $30,000 was allocated to an archaeological initiative directed by the president of Chinggis Khan University, founder of the Center for Mongolian Historical and Cultural Heritage. Launched in 2007, this initiative aimed at assessing and protecting historic monuments and archaeological sites surrounding Ulaanbaatar, including a Neolithic settlement and several Mongol graves dating from the twelfth century to the fourteenth century.

Starting in 2006, the Ambassadors Fund also supported the Mongolian Monasteries Documentation Project. Relying heavily on GPS technology, the intent was to map, photograph, and document Mongolian monasteries destroyed during the 1930s. The effort also involved collecting oral histories dating to that period.

Finally, the US embassy is playing a notable part in helping to preserve and protect the early eighteenth-century Amarbayasgalant Monastery located in a remote but beautiful valley five hours north of Ulaanbaatar. At the urging of Ambassador Minton, an initial grant of $86,000 in 2009 involved an architectural survey and a fire safety and security assessment. One year later, Mongolia became one of only four countries worldwide to receive its first ever "large grant," totaling $586,000, under the Ambassadors Fund. (Other awardees that year included an Armenian church in Turkey, a Moghul hunting lodge in Pakistan, and an archaeological site in Afghanistan.) The grant for Mongolia is being used to help restore the roof of the Amarbayasgalant Monastery's main temple and protect it against damage from fire and theft.

As a rare survivor of the government-ordered destruction of Buddhist monasteries during the 1930s, Amarbayasgalant is a site of increasing interest, as both a pilgrimage site and a tourist destination. It is also closely associated with Zanabazar, the Mongolian Buddhist cultural figure who established the monastery, created some of Mongolia's most famous sculptures, and designed the *soyombo* symbol that now appears in the Mongolian flag.

As with other Foreign Service officers serving in Mongolia, I have found that personal experience with those involved in cultural preservation provides important opportunities to deepen engagement with Mongolians from all walks of life. In particular, the Amarbayasgalant grant ensured that the US embassy was well represented at a ceremony to mark the opening of a large new stupa at the monastery in August 2010.

Remarkably, the guest of honor at that ceremony, held just outside Amarbayasgalant monastery, was an elderly lama who, as a young monk back in the 1930s, had witnessed the very moment when the monastery was closed, the older lamas were shot or imprisoned, and the younger monks were forced to join the military. In a moving way, the ceremony acknowledged the pain of Mongolia's past while also affirming the continued renewal of a more ancient Buddhist tradition at one of the country's most important religious sites.

****

Other types of cultural exchanges enrich the US-Mongolian relationship. On a private basis, individual artists have traveled back and forth between the two countries, using their own funds or those provided by private foundations. Unique aspects of Mongolian culture—including both throat singing and the *morin huur*—typically find appreciative audiences across the United States. Over the last two decades, various genres of American popular music such as rock, hip-hop, and jazz have also influenced contemporary music development in Mongolia.

According to at least one account, the first officially funded cultural visit by an American performer to Mongolia occurred in 1989, followed a year later by the arrival of country and western singer Steve Young. Several years after that, in January 1995, the American jazz group Bela Fleck and the Flecktones visited Mongolia, playing to a sellout crowd at the Philharmonic Hall in Ulaanbaatar. The group reportedly blended a "dizzying assortment of influences, among them jazz, funk, blue grass, R&B, reggae, folk, and world music, into an 'accessible yet exhilarating fresh style.'" As is typically the case in such programs, efforts were made to include Mongolian music in the mix and the popular Mongolian pop singer Sarantuya also made an appearance.

Since that early concert, the embassy's Public Affairs section has sponsored a steady stream of other cultural visitors, including musicians representing a wide variety of genres, including jazz, classical, and hip-hop. The hip-hop group Opus Aboken performed in Darkhan; Erdenet was the venue for a concert by the classical trio Chicago and Friends; and Baganuur and Sukhbaatar welcomed the Ari

Roland Jazz Quartet. Modern dance became part of the mix in early 2000 when the embassy funded two professional modern dance teachers. In more recent years, dance companies from Chicago, New York, and Washington have performed in Mongolia.

Cultural traditions from the American West bear a special resemblance to Mongolia and have been part of the cultural interchange over the years. For example, in 2005 Ambassador Pamela Slutz made arrangements for a visit to Mongolia by members of the Western Folklife Center in Elko, Nevada. That same year, a delegation of Native Americans representing the Zuni, Navajo, and Apache tribes visited Mongolia, highlighting and affirming the many spiritual, cultural, and linguistic affinities that exist between Mongolia and certain Native American communities.

Perhaps the most significant and certainly the largest cultural event involving Americans and Mongolians thus far occurred in June 2010, when the Los Angeles–based, Grammy Award–winning hip-hop band Ozomatli visited Ulaanbaatar as part of a larger East Asian tour. Again, the musical influences were remarkably varied, reflecting the diversity of the United States and including not only hip-hop but also Latino salsa, New Orleans R&B, Jamaican reggae, and Indian raga. Ozomatli also conducted music workshops and included a special performance for disabled children on their program. The massive concluding concert held in Sukhbaatar Square was undoubtedly the highlight, filling central Ulaanbaatar and attracting an audience estimated to number as many as 25,000. The concert also featured the work of Mongolian musicians, highlighting again the unusual yet highly entertaining synthesis that often emerges when artistic figures from Mongolia and the United States meet, improvise, and learn from each other.

* * * * * * *

State Department cultural and educational initiatives make a further impact in areas such as journalism and publishing. One 2001 Visitor Program, for example, brought 12 Mongolian editors, press officers, and journalists to the United States. And a number of American journalists, including representatives from Voice of America (VOA), National Public Radio (NPR), Cable News Network (CNN), and Hearst Newspaper Syndicate have taught training courses in Mongolia over the years.

Public Affairs programming also helps support NGOs involved in the media, including Globe International, which plays a pioneering role in promoting freedom of information. With help from the embassy, Globe International organized a study tour to the United States and funded projects on topics such as "The Right to Know: Freedom of Information," "State Secrecy and Freedom of Information," and "Protecting the Journalists' Confidential Sources and Repealing the Criminal Defamatory Legislation," initiatives that have enriched the discussion within Mongolia on issues vital to journalists and the free flow of information. As a result of these and other programs, freedom of information is increasingly recognized as a public right and measures to promote it are now being discussed in parliament.

Another US-funded program supports the translation of English-language material into Mongolian. Most notably, in 2001 the embassy released the translation of *Basic Media Writing* by Melvin Mencher, a volume that now serves as the primary textbook for journalism students across Mongolia. Several prominent Mongolian journalists helped in the translation, including Ts. Enkhbat, director of TV 9, and B. Durevdash, director of Mongolian Public Radio.

More recently and largely at the initiative of Ambassador Mark Minton, the first *Anthology of American Poetry* translated into Mongolian was released in 2010, featuring works by contemporary American poets such as David Lehman, who has visited Mongolia, and classic American poets such as Walt Whitman, Emily Dickinson, Edgar Allen Poe, Stephen Crane, Robert Frost, Langston Hughes, and Allen Ginsberg. A second *Anthology of American Poetry* followed in late 2011. The well-known Mongolian poet Mend-Ooyo played a vital role in obtaining needed copyrights and bringing both sets of translations into print.

* * * * * * *

The most durable and sustained cultural impact often comes in the form of partnerships forged with specific institutions that take a long-term perspective and can be sustained over long periods of time. As an independent entity, the Arts Council of Mongolia has already made important contributions in cultivating and promoting the arts in Mongolia. The initial idea to establish the Council was an outgrowth of an early exchange program involving a two-week intensive study tour of the United States in 2000, organized by the embassy's Public Affairs section, in which five Mongolian art managers participated.

Two years later, with additional support from the Open Society Forum, a pioneering group of Mongolian arts, civic, and business leaders formed the Arts Council of Mongolia, or ACM as it is usually known. A subsequent partnership developed with the Seattle Arts Council in the state of Washington, which provides further technical and financial support while also strengthening cultural relations between Mongolia and the United States.

Indeed, the ACM has been the implementing agency for several grants under the Ambassador's Cultural Preservation Fund, including the most recent large grant to the Amarbayasgalant Monastery. Over the years, ACM has expanded its support base to include other embassies as well as private companies. Nonetheless, the US embassy remains vitally involved.

The American Center for Mongolian Studies (ACMS) is another institution that has made important contributions toward strengthening relations between the United States and Mongolia over many years. In this case, the emphasis is on facilitating opportunities for American scholars to study in Mongolia. The role of ACMS has increased as more scholars have become interested in Mongolia as a focal point of their research. While ACMS numbers two dozen major American academic institutions among its members, its base of support has in recent years expanded to include universities and research centers in both Russia and Canada.

ACMS opened its Ulaanbaatar office and library in spring 2004. Originally based at Western Washington University, the ACMS office in the United States is now hosted by the University of Wisconsin in Madison. The Ulaanbaatar ACMS office maintains a library featuring more than 3,000 books on Mongolia, currently housed at the Mongolian University of Science and Technology in its "e-learning" building. Interestingly, Charles Krusekopf—the first executive director of ACMS—served as an intern at the US embassy in Ulaanbaatar in 1992.

The growing network of other ACMS supporters includes private American citizens and major institutional donors such as the Open Society Institute (Soros Foundation). In addition, US government grants to ACMS over the years have included grants from the Department of State, the Department of Education, and the US embassy in Ulaanbaatar.

Increasingly, the ACMS library in Ulaanbaatar is used by local Mongolians as well as visiting students and academics from the United States and elsewhere, including Fulbright scholars. ACMS itself has raised more than $400,000 for American and Mongolian students to pursue their research in Mongolian studies in Mongolia.

Over the years, ACMS has organized dozens of public lectures and a variety of workshops and conferences. Most notably, as a full member of the Council of American Overseas Research Centers (and its only member in Northeast and Central Asia), ACMS hosted an international gathering of representatives from 23 other member research institutions in August 2011, thus providing leading academics from across the United States and around the world their first opportunity to visit Mongolia.

Here again, private efforts often have an even broader impact. During 2012, the Genghis Khan exhibit—organized by "Dino Don" Lessem and using artifacts loaned from public and private collections in Russia, Mongolia, the United States, and elsewhere—was displayed to appreciative audiences at the Field Museum in Chicago, after touring in Texas, Colorado, California, and North Carolina and providing many hundreds of thousands of Americans a firsthand look at the enduring legacy of the Mongol empire. As the exhibit's efforts to draw links between the past and the present enhanced its interest, at least some of those who paid to see the exhibit are likely to be intrigued enough to eventually visit Mongolia for themselves.

In another context, sister-to-sister partnerships are yet one more mechanism that has proved helpful in people-to-people ties between citizens of the United States and Mongolia over the years. The Denver-Ulaanbaatar sister city relationship is especially notable. Its tenth anniversary celebrations during the summer of 2011 brought both private citizens and government officials from Denver to Ulaanbaatar, including Jim Wagenlander, the honorary Mongolian consul in Colorado. In recognition of the Denver-Ulaanbaatar sister city partnership, the street along the Selbe River on which the US embassy is located, was officially renamed "Denver Street." As one outgrowth of the partnership between Mongolia and the state of Colorado, the Denver Zoo developed its own relationship, in this case with the Ikh Nart nature reserve south of Choir, home to relatively large numbers of ibex and argali sheep.

Other sister city relationships have been developed over the years, including one linking Erdenet with Fairbanks, Alaska, and another linking Tsetserleg with Bellingham, Washington. Still other prospective sister city relationships are currently under discussion and likely to move forward in the years ahead.

****

Perhaps no US-sponsored program in Mongolia reflects the strength and enduring power of people-to-people relationships better than the Peace Corps. The basic framework was set in Ulaanbaatar on August 2, 1990, when Secretary of State James Baker and Minister of Foreign Affairs Gombosuren signed the foundational agreement leading to the establishment of a Peace Corps program in Mongolia. Since that time, well over 800 Americans have undertaken Peace Corps assignments in Mongolia, many of them serving in some of the most remote corners of the country.

In Mongolia, as in any country, the goal of the Peace Corps is threefold: to provide training in high priority areas such as health, education, and business development; to promote a better understanding of the United States in the countries to which Peace Corps Volunteers are assigned; and to help the Americans assigned as volunteers to better understand the countries in which they serve.

Officially, the Peace Corps opened its doors in Mongolia in January 1991, when Chuck Howell arrived in Ulaanbaatar with his young family to serve as the first country director. Approximately six months later—on July 3, 1991—the first group of Peace Corps Volunteers, numbering 21, arrived in Mongolia to take up their assignments after a long flight from the United States to Beijing followed by a 36-hour train ride to Ulaanbaatar. All 21 were assigned to sites in Ulaanbaatar. According to Ambassador Lake, "The initial Peace Corps group was tremendously successful."

Early areas of emphasis included English language instruction, computer skills training, and business development. In 1992, a new group of 25 Peace Corps Volunteers arrived, some taking on assignments outside the capital, including in Darkhan, Orkhon, Selenge, Ovorhangai, Dundgovi, Omnogobi, Sukhbaatar, and Henti.

The 1992 volunteers had been deliberately placed within one overnight's drive from Ulaanbaatar. Gasoline at the time was not always available, so the Peace Corps put a 50-gallon drum of gasoline at each location to ensure that, if necessary, volunteers could be brought to Ulaanbaatar quickly. During subsequent years, the Peace Corps reach expanded still further into the countryside, and volunteers were soon living and working in *aimags* and *soums* across the length and breadth of Mongolia.

In relation to the size of Mongolia's population, the Peace Corps program by 2010 ranked proportionately as one of the largest in the world. In August 2011, a further 66 Peace Corps Volunteers were sworn in following the completion of their training program in Darkhan, north of Ulaanbaatar. This brought the total number of in-country volunteers to 135—the largest number ever.

Visits by senior Peace Corps officials over the years reflect the importance of the Peace Corps program in Mongolia. For example, in June 1996, Peace Corps Director Mark Gearan traveled to Mongolia, meeting with Prime Minister Elbegdorj. Similarly, in April 2007 Peace Corps Director Ron Tschetter visited President Enkhbayar. Both senior visitors also met with Peace Corps Volunteers and were introduced to Mongolian counterparts from around the country.

English language teaching was a major focus from the very beginning and remains the single largest Peace Corps program in Mongolia to this day. The intent is to improve the skills of qualified Mongolian English language teachers, develop English resources materials, and work directly with students to improve their English language skills. By 2011, some 580 Peace Corps Volunteers had taught English in Mongolia at one time or another, most having been assigned to secondary schools, provincial education departments, or institutes of higher education in settlements across the country.

Over the years, the program has developed other areas of interest and activity, including computer training, health education, community economic development, youth development, and the environment. Establishing and sustaining strong relationships with local counterparts has always been a central part of the Peace Corps program in Mongolia. Typically, host institutions not only offer a useful work setting but also provide housing. While some Peace Corps Volunteers live in apartments, many experience traditional Mongolian culture firsthand by living in *gers* throughout their two-year Peace Corps assignment.

On occasion, Peace Corps Volunteers have assumed assignments that help further strengthen the impact of other US-funded programs. For example, individual Peace Corps Volunteers recently helped counterparts develop proposals for Millennium Challenge Agency "small grant" programs in the health sector. Similarly, Peace Corps Volunteers have worked with the USAID-funded Ger and Gobi initiatives and with Mongolian entities that had previously received USAID support, such as Development Solutions and Khaan Bank.

"Secondary projects" constitute another important feature of the Peace Corps program in Mongolia. While making significant contributions throughout their "primary" assignments, volunteers each select and develop a specific community outreach project at some point during their two years of service in Mongolia. These projects help expand the impact of the Peace Corps presence still further.

Over the last two decades, secondary projects undertaken by Peace Corps Volunteers have been the catalyst for countless workshops, seminars, and new Websites; helped establish new libraries, information centers, and computer labs; and contributed to the publication of new curricula, guidebooks, brochures, training manuals, and even Mongolia's first sign language dictionary. During their time in Mongolia, individual Peace Corps Volunteers have formed clubs, composed music, organized rock bands, built greenhouses, produced public awareness videos, launched television shows, helped disabled people, equipped libraries, donated bikes, and provided helmets for young Mongolian jockeys racing in local *Naadam* festivals.

While Peace Corps Volunteers typically work in Mongolia for two years, the experience of life on the steppe remains with them for a lifetime. When they return to the United States, they bring with them a wealth of knowledge and personal experience about Mongolia—and are well positioned to pass that knowledge and experience on to friends, families, and communities back home. During training, each Peace Corps Volunteer is assigned a "host family"; and, once assigned, each volunteer is paired with a Mongolian counterpart. Often, these key relationships mark the start of lifelong personal and family friendships involving Peace Corps Volunteers and the individual Mongolians with whom they live and work.

As the number of Mongolians living in the United States grows, contacts are often made in both directions. It is not unusual to find Americans—often returned Peace Corps Volunteers—joining with local Mongolians to participate in a local mini *Naadam, Tsagaan Sar,* or other celebration. Some also find romance during their Peace Corps assignment and end up marrying Mongolians or fellow Peace Corps Volunteers.

Beginning with the arrival of the first Peace Corps class in 1991, Peace Corps Volunteers have made an impact in a variety of professions, ranging from private business to education to government service. For example, several returned Peace Corps Volunteers from Mongolia now serve in USAID and the State Department as Foreign Service officers. Others are engaged in international work in various NGOs such as the Academy for Educational Development (AED) or the International Rescue Committee (IRC).

Following their Peace Corps assignment more than a few volunteers find ways to stay directly involved in Mongolia. Some have returned to work at the embassy or in the Peace Corps offices in Ulaanbaatar. Others continue to teach English in Mongolia, some at high schools and universities in Ulaanbaatar. Still others have applied their skills with local and international NGOs such as Pact, Mercy Corps, and the Asia Foundation.

Over the years, some former Peace Corps Volunteers have returned to Mongolia to find employment in the country's rapidly growing private sector, in at least one case in a senior executive position with a major international mining company. Whatever the setting, experience gained as the result of a Peace Corps assignment in Mongolia is often highly rewarding, both personally and professionally.

Returned Peace Corps Volunteers were also the catalyst in creating Friends of Mongolia, a US-based NGO incorporated as a nonprofit organization in New York in 1999. Founded by the seventh group of volunteers ("M-7s") to serve in Mongolia, the organization helps to sustain a continued interest in Mongolia long after those working there have departed. The Friends of Mongolia Facebook page now has more than 1,500 members, indicating that interest in Mongolia goes far beyond returned Peace Corps volunteers.

Friends of Mongolia aims in part to spread awareness about Mongolia in the United States. At the same time, it also supports projects in Mongolia, in part by funding innovative community initiatives and providing scholarships for Mongolians from rural families to study in Ulaanbaatar. During the 2010–11 school year, Friends of Mongolia funded 13 such scholarships and assisted with an additional 12 Matthew Girvin memorial scholarships. Matthew Girvin was an American aid worker employed by UNICEF as part of a UN *dzud* team who was killed in a helicopter crash in western Mongolia in January 2001. His parents established the scholarship fund after his death to honor both his memory and his commitment to Mongolia.

In a very tangible way, organizations such as Friends of Mongolia and initiatives such as the Mathew Girvin memorial scholarship fund further deepen and strengthen people-to-people ties. They also support the aim of many individual Americans to become a "most helpful factor in the development of a wonderful country."

Chapter 8
Looking Ahead

"God has placed in every human heart the desire to be free."

In mid-June 2011, following in the footsteps of his immediate predecessors Ochirbat (1993–97), Bagabandai (1997–2005), and Enkhbayar (2005–08), all of whom had met with serving American presidents, President Elbegdorj traveled to Washington to meet with President Obama at the White House.

His trip to the United States lasted most of the week. It started in San Francisco, where he met the mayor, visited The Asia Foundation and the Asia Museum, spoke at Stanford University, and held a dialogue with members of the Mongolian American community living in the Bay area. He also officially opened the new Mongolian Consulate in San Francisco, an important step that should help further strengthen Mongolia's profile in the western United States. Several days later, President Elbegdorj concluded his American journey in New York, where he spoke to the Council on Foreign Relations and was interviewed by various members of the press.

In between, the wide range of activities arranged during his two-day stay at Blair House in Washington reflected the depth and breadth of the expanding US-Mongolian partnership over nearly 25 years. While the Oval Office meeting was the highlight of the journey, other stops in Washington underscored the comprehensive and growing nature of the diplomatic relationship.

Having studied at the University of Colorado and at Harvard University's Kennedy School, President Elbegdorj was well aware of the symbolism associated with many of the events on his itinerary. For example, he began his first day in Washington by laying a wreath at the Tomb of the Unknown Soldier in Arlington Cemetery, accompanied by his wife and youngest son, who was born in Massachusetts around the same time as the 9/11 attacks on the Pentagon and New York's World Trade Center in 2001. From there, he proceeded to Walter Reed Hospital, meeting with wounded American soldiers and delivering handwritten greeting cards prepared by his 24 foster children back in Ulaanbaatar.

President Elbegdorj was accompanied on his visit to both Arlington Cemetery and Walter Reed by Sergeant Azzaya and Sergeant Samuu-Yondon, the two Mongolian NCOs who had demonstrated conspicuous bravery in foiling the plans of a would-be suicide bomber during the Mongolian military's second rotation in Iraq. Later, he was joined at Blair House by Minister of Defense Bold in a meeting with Admiral Michael Mullen, chairman of the Joint Chiefs of Staff, providing another opportunity to discuss the evolution of Mongolia's military over the past many years, including not only its current deployment in Afghanistan but also its growing role in UN peacekeeping operations throughout the world.

Other aspects of the visit emphasized Mongolia's growing commercial ties with the United States and its commitment to democracy. During his time in Washington, President Elbegdorj addressed a large group of business leaders at a lunch sponsored by the American Chamber of Commerce; witnessed new agreements with the Department of Commerce and Federal Aviation Authority; observed the signing of documents to formalize the sale of three Boeing aircraft to Mongolia; and was hosted at another lunch by Secretary of Commerce Gary Locke, an American of Chinese origin who would shortly depart as the new United States ambassador to Beijing.

Democracy themes also figured prominently in the visit, for example in a speech at the Brookings Institution and in meetings on Capitol Hill with the leadership of the Senate and the House of Representatives. At a lecture at the US Capitol sponsored by the Congressional Mongolian Caucus with the House Democracy Partnership and the National Endowment for Democracy, President Elbegdorj reflected at length on "shared" values, repeating more than once the statement that democracy is truly a Mongolian value and that Mongolians, too, desire to decide for themselves where they live, what they believe, how they worship and what they want to think and say. Reflecting further, at one point he suggested, "God has placed in every human heart the desire to be free."

On one evening, the Mongolian embassy hosted a reception at a restaurant overlooking the Mall, the Washington Monument, and the US Capitol. The event started with two national anthems—one a praise song to the Mongolian homeland, the other the "Star Spangled Banner," both delivered in the haunting, high voice of a Mongolian long song singer.

In another evening event, this one sponsored by the Asia Society, President Elbegdorj received the group's "Distinguished Statesman Award," after which Dr. Henry Kissinger received the Asia Society's "Lifetime Achievement Award." Two other awards were presented that night—one, on "Public Policy," to Under Secretary of the Treasury Lael Brainard, the other, on "International Business," to Jim Rogers from the United States and Wang Yusuo from China. The evening entertainment included a *tsam* "mask dance," provided by the Mongolian Khan Bogd ensemble directed by Gankhuyag Natsag. In addition, the bilingual Yu Ying ("nurturing excellence") charter school, located in Washington, performed a familiar Chinese song and dance for the large and appreciative audience.

In possibly unintentional ways, the juxtaposition of themes related to Mongolia and China at the Asia Society dinner, as well as the presence of Henry Kissinger as an acclaimed twentieth-century foreign policy strategist, accentuated the changing face of Asia, while also underscoring some of the major new challenges that lay ahead. More than a decade into the twenty-first century, East Asia is becoming increasingly visible while undergoing significant change. Mongolia too, with one foot in Northeast Asia and another in Central Asia, is part of this mix and faces a period of both great challenge and incredible opportunity. If Mongolia has already witnessed dramatic events and great change during the past 25 years, the next quarter century promises to be at least as interesting.

****

What form will US-Mongolian diplomatic relations take in the coming years? While predictions are inherently risky, there is little doubt that a strong foundation has been established, one that is both broad and deep. In January 1987, when diplomatic notes were signed at the Department of State leading to the establishment of new embassies in Washington and Ulaanbaatar, Mongolia was almost as isolated as North Korea is now. Yet, in just 25 years, Mongolia has maintained good relations with its neighbors while reaching out to the wider world. It has also fundamentally transformed the way in which it is governed as well as the organizing principles on which its economy and society are based.

As a country, Mongolia has changed fundamentally. It is wealthier than it used to be; and, as a society, it has become far more complex. During the 1990s, many Mongolians had high hopes for democracy and its anticipated material benefits. Mongolians also reveled in rediscovering their identity and history, which had been suppressed during the Soviet era. By 2012, Mongolians had become more nationalistic, more cynical about their politicians, and more skeptical about the intentions and motivations of foreign investors attracted by the country's mining boom. At the same time, Mongolians have become more religious in some cases, due partly to a modest revival in religious belief and practice derived in part from Tibetan Buddhism and from visits involving Buddhist spiritual leaders in recent years. These included a visit by the Dalai Lama in late 2011 in which he urged his followers to "learn English" in order to forge closer ties with the wider world. While Tibetan Buddhism plays an increasingly notable role in Mongolia, the Kazakh Muslim minority in the far west and in Ulaanbaatar and a newer Christian presence in some parts of the country are also now a part of the Mongolian religious and social fabric. Inevitably, these changes in Mongolia's economy and society will have an impact on the way in which the United States and Mongolia interact in the years ahead.

Looking beyond 2012, there should certainly be opportunities for the US-Mongolian diplomatic partnership to be strengthened still further, not only through bilateral co-operation but also by deepened engagement in multilateral forums. Increasingly, what were once perceived as isolated, country-specific issues are becoming more regional, even global, in scope. Common interests will come into play, and common values will further enrich the discussion. If Mongolia ultimately succeeds in its aim of becoming a truly successful market-based democracy, its experience will provide important, relevant "lessons learned" in Asia and beyond.

Development ties between the United States and Mongolia, involving ongoing partnerships with both USAID and MCC, are important now but, it is hoped, will fade into history over the next 25 years, or possibly within the next decade, if not earlier. Indeed, Mongolia will be in a much better place when vibrant and flourishing commercial ties, rather than foreign aid, determine its development path. Just as South Korea was transformed from an aid-receiving to an aid-giving country in little more than a generation, Mongolia too could aspire to such change.

International experience related to the growth and expansion of mineral-rich economies is sobering. Much of this experience is well known in Mongolia. Among other things, it emphasizes the importance of focusing on major long-term priorities, most notably education, infrastructure, and good governance. Tackling corruption is another vital issue, as is ensuring that social and environmental concerns be properly addressed. No two issues are more important for Mongolia than instilling good governance and reducing corruption. If these twin concerns are not effectively addressed, all of Mongolia's other dreams for the future could come crashing down.

Drawing on widely available international experience from many countries, Mongolia will want to implement approaches that minimize the "boom or bust" nature of mineral price cycles, in part by diversifying its own economy. While the mining sector will be central in shaping Mongolia's future, other sectors such as tourism, agriculture, and services also offer important avenues for future success.

One hopes that commercial ties between Mongolian and American companies will grow significantly during the coming years. In addition to technology, US companies bring knowledge of hard-earned lessons in how to address environmental, social, and other concerns. Subject to the prohibitions of the Foreign Corrupt Practices Act, the American business community also provides a level of transparency, accountability, and corporate governance that is not universally observed. As Mongolia moves forward, the quality of the private firms operating in the country will be at least as important as the magnitude of the foreign investment it attracts.

At this point, direct US private investment in Mongolia remains at modest, even disappointing levels. In the coming years, one hopes it will increase substantially, building and strengthening a vibrant economic relationship to complement those already established in other areas. Realistically, in the absence of a strong commercial partnership involving not only trade but also investment between the two countries, it is hard to see how relations in other areas can thrive over the long term.

National sovereignty is the central concern of any government, and security requirements will continue to be viewed by senior Mongolian officials as an important issue in the years ahead. At some level, Mongolia has survived in the past by being seen as "the sharp bone that no one else would ever want to swallow." Given its geographic location, Mongolia is irrevocably connected with both Russia to the north and China to the south. Inevitably, important aspects of Mongolia's future will depend on what happens in both countries in ways almost entirely beyond Mongolia's control. Demographic or other decline in Russia and rising nationalism among a younger generation in China would both have negative repercussions for Mongolia. Economic problems in either country would also adversely affect Mongolia.

As Mongolia faces continued rapid change, it will look even more deeply into its own past to strengthen its identity, drawing on age-old cultural and spiritual resources when confronting an uncertain and increasingly unfamiliar future. In the past Mongolia's strong sense of self-identity, combined with an ability to respond calmly to outside challenges with flexibility and pragmatism, have always been among its main strengths. At its best, Mongolia as a society will reflect a strong sense of self-confidence while engaging in positive ways with the rest of the world. More pessimistically, the emergence of latent xenophobic tendencies in Mongolia, as in all societies, could undermine relations with its neighbors both near and far.

As Mongolia's strategic approach over the last two decades suggests, security in an increasingly globalized world made up of nations large and small inherently involves at least two main tasks. First, it requires maintaining internal strength and cohesion rather than displaying a divided face to the wider world. And, second, it requires a strong commitment to dealing with the outside world in a positive and proactive way, typically involving mutual co-operation as part of joint efforts that include many other countries. Mongolia's participation in UN peacekeeping assignments in Africa and elsewhere has added significantly to its international reputation. Such deployments will likely become even more visible and possibly more frequent in the future.

The need for national consensus necessarily places a strong burden on Mongolian politicians. While engaging in vocal and sometimes acrimonious and even ferocious debate on internal issues, they will need to present a unified face to the rest of the world, at least regarding the main pillars of the country's foreign policy. Mongolia's current approach to foreign policy, based on strong ties with its first and second neighbors while reaching out to a diverse set of "third neighbors," is a powerful formulation. Ironically, the more successful that Mongolia is in doing this, the harder it will become.

The generally high level of goodwill that Mongolia enjoys on the international stage, will, it is hoped, make the process easier. In early 2011, *National Geographic* ranked Mongolia among the "top 20" travel destinations of the year. Also in 2011, CNN described Mongolians as one of the "top ten coolest nationalities," somewhat behind countries such as Brazil and Jamaica and ahead of the United States. The *New York Times* ranked Mongolia high on a similar list of top travel destinations published in early 2013. A few years ago, the founder of the Mongol state—Genghis Khan—was declared as none other than "Man of the Millennium." Very probably, Mongolia will continue to figure in similar rankings related to tourism, culture, history, and other topics in the years ahead.

Such rankings are not scientifically based and need not be taken too seriously. More to the point, Mongolia should be more interested in where it ranks on Transparency International's Corruption Perceptions Index or on any number of "ease of doing business" or "level of innovation" indexes, areas in which Mongolia's performance has been mixed in recent years. That said, international reputation can make a difference. A country with unique cultural features and strong "brand recognition" is better placed to thrive in a connected world in which former notions of geographic isolation are becoming much less relevant.

At this point, Mongolia's "soft power" as viewed from North America and Europe lies to a considerable extent on its reputation as a faraway exotic place that provides a convenient platform on which others all too often project their own myths and fantasies. In an increasingly homogenized world, those living in other countries will usually find most attractive the distinctive aspects of Mongolia. The sense of spaciousness that Mongolia's wide-open spaces make possible strikes an especially evocative chord, and one hopes it will be maintained, whatever lies ahead.

If Mongolia is "lucky," it could emerge as a country like Australia, a relatively egalitarian society shaped by the ethos of the outback, even if most of its citizens do not live there. The next generation of Mongolians will face many choices and, for many, the realities of life in a small town or as part of a herder encampment that moves four times each year do not figure in their plans for the future. For them, the bright lights of a big city like Ulaanbaatar (or Tokyo, Seoul, or Los Angeles, for that matter) beckon and can become overwhelming.

Yet it is hard to imagine a Mongolia in which nomadic traditions do not play an essential part in shaping and forming the wider society—and where herders are not perceived in some measure as serving as the "guardians of the nation's soul." Certainly, friends of Mongolia around the world will wish Mongolia well as it seeks to preserve this aspect of the country, even if most of Mongolia's citizens live in Ulaanbaatar and other cities and towns rather than being scattered across the vast countryside. Already, more Mongolians live in urban areas than in rural areas, and this trend is likely to continue for at least the next several years, in keeping with similar transitions that have taken place in other parts of the world.

Maintaining a positive international reputation will hinge partly on Mongolia's ability to retain the distinctive aspects of its culture while also keeping its commitment to democracy. In addition, it will want to address environmental concerns in ways that ensure that the magnificent Mongolian countryside remains largely protected. Amidst the enormous changes now underway across the country, sympathetic outside observers will fervently hope that Mongolia can somehow also manage to maintain the ethos of the steppe, one based on centuries of history and a herding lifestyle that so far has met the test of time and proved both resilient and sustainable, even if the various forms it takes have changed over time.

Along with commercial relations, strong people-to-people ties also represent a potential area of further strength in the US-Mongolia partnership. Already, the growing number of Mongolians enrolled at colleges and universities in the United States, who then return to Mongolia on completion of their studies, bodes well for the future. During the coming years, the number of Mongolians studying in the United States will likely increase still further, even as more and more Americans find their way to Mongolia, whether as students, tourists, academics, or entrepreneurs. Alumni ties that last a lifetime will further strengthen the relationship. And at some point, there may well be a thriving American University in Mongolia—perhaps more than one.

Beyond education, Mongolia's intriguing cultural assets, fascinating history, and unique landscapes should help build ties still further in the years ahead. Whether involving creative artists, academic researchers, or environmental NGOs, there is significant scope for Mongolians and Americans to study and work together while also learning from each other. Governments can certainly aid and facilitate this effort. But, over the long term, the most compelling and durable people-to-people ties are typically those that have been established and sustained without bureaucratic interference. More usually, it is private individuals working creatively, independently, and on their own, who are able to build and maintain the most enduring people-to-people relations.

Looking back, those directly involved in first launching diplomatic ties between the United States and Mongolia in January 1987 could hardly have contemplated just how far the relationship might travel in the next quarter century. Looking ahead another 25 years, to January 2037 when, it is hoped, the first half-century of the US-Mongolian partnership will be celebrated with appropriate toasts and fireworks, the shape of the future may seem even more unimaginable.

Yet, in navigating the obstacles as well as the opportunities that undoubtedly lie ahead, it will almost certainly be useful to occasionally recall an earlier American diplomat's words about Mongolia. That short phrase, written by A. W. Ferrin to his colleagues back at the State Department in Washington in 1918, expressed the hope that, having established a formal diplomatic presence in Ulaanbaatar, the United States might indeed prove to be a "*most helpful factor in the development of a wonderful country.*"

Annexes

Key Agreements between the United States and Mongolia, 1987–2012

Memorandum of Understanding between the Government of the United States of America and the Government of the Mongolian People's Republic Concerning Facilitation of the Work of Diplomatic Missions (January 27, 1987)

Agreement for Cooperation in Cultural and Educational Exchange between the Government of the United States of America and the Government of the Mongolian People's Republic (September 29, 1989)

Agreement on Cooperation between the Government of the United States of America and the Government of the Mongolian People's Republic through the United States Peace Corps in the Mongolian People's Republic (August 2, 1990)

Investment Incentive Agreement (September 29, 1990)

Agreement on Trade Relations (January 23, 1991)

Memorandum of Understanding Concerning Facilitation of the Work of Diplomatic Missions (March 27, 1992)

Agreement between the Government of the United States of America and the Government of Mongolia Concerning Economic, Technical and Related Assistance (September 8, 1992)

Treaty between the United States of America and Mongolia Concerning the Encouragement and Reciprocal Protection of Investment (October 6, 1994)

Agreement Regarding Cooperation and Mutual Assistance in Customs Matters (June 19, 1996)

Agreement on Military Exchanges and Visits between the Government of the United States of America and the Government of Mongolia (June 26, 1996)

Agreement for Cooperation in the Global Learning and Observation to Benefit the Environment (GLOBE) Program (May 6, 1997)

Agreement Concerning the Employment of Dependents of Official Government Employees (April 5, 1999)

Memorandum of Understanding Concerning Scientific and Technical Cooperation in the Earth Sciences (April 2/June 26, 2003)

Joint Statement on Bilateral and Regional Cooperation (January 31, 2004)

Basic Exchange and Cooperative Agreement Concerning Geospatial Information and Services Cooperation (March 22, 2004)

Agreement Concerning the International School of Ulaanbaatar (May 26, 2004)

Joint Statement between the United States and Mongolia (July 15, 2004)

Millennium Challenge Compact between the United States of America Acting through the Millennium Challenge Corporation and the Government of Mongolia (October 22, 2007)

Cooperation to Suppress the Proliferation of Weapons of Mass Destruction, Their Delivery Systems and Related Materials by Sea (October 23, 2007)

Joint Statement on Expansion of Educational Exchanges between the United States and Ministry of Education, Culture and Science of Mongolia (January 25, 2010)

Memorandum of Understanding between the Government of the United States of America and the Government of Mongolia on Cooperation in the Field of Peaceful Uses of Nuclear Energy (September 22, 2010)

Joint Statement between the United States and Mongolia Following the Meeting between President Obama and President Elbegdorj at the White House (June 16, 2011)

US Ambassadors and Heads of Agencies in Mongolia, 1987–2012

Ambassadors

Richard Williams, 1988–90
Joseph Lake, 1990–93
Donald Johnson, 1993–96
Alphonse La Porta, 1997–2000
John Dinger, 2000–03
Pamela Slutz, 2003–06
Mark Minton, 2006–09
Jonathan Addleton, 2009–12
Piper Campbell, 2012–present

Peace Corps Directors

Chuck Howell, 1991–93
Jean Mead, 1993–96
Mark Zober, 1996–98
Rob Schexnayder, 1998–2001
Ken Heldenfeld, 2001–03
Helen Lowman, 2003–04
Carol Chappell, 2004
Ken Goodson, 2005–07
Jim Carl, 2007–2010
Ellen Paquetta, 2010–12
Darlene Grant, 2012–present

USAID Directors

Robert Friedline, 1991–92
Bill Nance, 1992–94
Chuck Howell, 1995–96
Ed Birgells, 1997–2001
Jonathan Addleton, 2001–04
Skip Waskin, 2004–06
Barry Primm, 2006–09
Chuck Howell, 2009–11
Frank Donovan, 2012–present

MCC Country Director

Robert Reid, 2008–present

Defense Attachés

Major John Baker, 1999–2001
Lt. Col. Tom Wilhelm, 2001–03
Lt. Col. Mark Gillette, 2003–06
Lt. Col. Antonio Chow, 2006–07
Lt. Col. Matthew Schwab, 2007–08
Lt. Col. David Tatman, 2008–10
Lt. Col. Jonathan Lau, 2010–present

U.S.-Mongolia Joint Statement Issued at the White House June 16, 2011

The President of the United States, Barack Obama, and the President of Mongolia, Elbegdorj Tsakhia, today reaffirmed their commitment to a United States–Mongolia comprehensive partnership based on common values and shared strategic interests. They emphasized their countries' common interest in protecting and promoting freedom, democracy and human rights worldwide, and continued their intention to strengthen trade, investment and people-to-people ties so as to support economic growth and deepen the bonds of friendship between their two peoples. The two sides underscored their commitment to promoting a peaceful, stable and prosperous Asia-Pacific region through closer regional cooperation and support for regional multilateral institutions.

The United States and Mongolia reaffirmed their nations' commitment to the principles of cooperation outlined in the 2007 U.S.-Mongolia Joint Statement, and to the consensus reached in the 2004 and 2005 U.S.-Mongolian Joint Statements. The United States applauded the progress made by the Mongolian people in the past 22 years to deepen the foundations of their young democracy, congratulated Mongolia on assuming the Chairmanship of the Community of Democracies in July 2011, and expressed its full support and close cooperation with Mongolia in successfully fulfilling the Chair's responsibilities.

Mongolia welcomed and supported the key role played by the United States as an Asia-Pacific nation in securing peace, stability and prosperity in the region. The United States reaffirmed its support for a secure and prosperous Mongolia that plays an active role in regional affairs and that promotes strong, friendly and open relations with its neighbors. The United States and Mongolia pledged to work together to address their shared economic, security and development interests through regional institutions in the Asia-Pacific and through the United Nations and other multilateral organizations.

The two sides committed to further develop their countries' strong economic partnership. The United States confirmed its support for Mongolia's efforts to integrate its economy into regional and international economic and financial institutions. Mongolia expressed its appreciation for continued U.S. support and economic assistance. Mongolia noted the important role that U.S. companies, with their internationally leading management, technical, safety, environmental and sustainable mining practices, will play in the development of the country's coal, other mineral resources, infrastructure, agriculture, energy and tourism industries. The United States welcomed Mongolian International Airlines' decision to purchase Boeing commercial jetliners and its declared intention to expand its fleet further with U.S. aircraft in the future. The United States and Mongolia expressed their intention to ensure a welcoming investment and business climate for each other's companies. In this regard, the two sides highlighted the importance of concluding the negotiations and signing a bilateral Transparency Agreement by the end of 2011, taking into full account the resources, capacity and legal processes of each country. In order to further deepen economic ties, the two sides signed additional memoranda aimed at trade promotion and aviation cooperation.

Mongolia expressed its thanks for the support provided by the United States under the Millennium Challenge Corporation Compact Agreement, and both sides looked forward to the continued successful implementation of Compact projects that will increase transparency, stimulate sustained economic growth and alleviate poverty in Mongolia. The Mongolian side expressed its intention to take the necessary steps to qualify for consideration for a second MCC Compact Agreement.

The United States thanked Mongolia for its support of the international coalition in Afghanistan, for its announced intention to re-deploy peacekeeping forces to Iraq, and for the country's notable support for UN peacekeeping efforts in Africa. Mongolia thanked the United States for the support it provided to Mongolia's Defense Reform Program. As part of this effort, the nations are working together to build an air mobility capability to support peacekeeping and humanitarian assistance operations. Both sides decided to continue practical cooperation in peacekeeping training through exercises such as Gobi Wolf, Khaan Quest and Pacific Angel.

The United States and Mongolia have decided to explore mutually advantageous activities in nuclear energy based on the September 2010 Memorandum of Understanding between the two countries. The United States recognized and supported the Mongolian Nuclear Initiative, and applauded Mongolia's nuclear weapons free status. Mongolia confirmed its support for President Obama's Prague vision to include the call for a "New International Framework."

The United States and Mongolia expressed their intention to deepen and broaden people-to-people ties. Building on the creativity of our societies, both countries emphasized the importance that educational and cultural exchanges play in the bilateral relationship, and confirmed the role that innovative public-private partnerships can play in strengthening bilateral ties.

U.S. Senate Resolution on Mongolia Sponsored by Senators Kerry, McCain, Murkowski, and Webb June 17, 2011

Expressing the sense of the Senate regarding Mongolian President Tsakhiagiin Elbegdorj's visit to Washington, DC, and its support for the growing partnership between the United States and Mongolia.

Whereas the United States Government established diplomatic relations with the Government of Mongolia in January 1987, followed by the opening of a United States Embassy in Ulaanbaatar in June 1988;

Whereas in 1990, the Government of Mongolia declared an end to one-party Communist rule and initiated lasting democratic and free market reforms;

Whereas the United States Government has a longstanding commitment, based on its interests and values, to encouraging economic and political reforms in Mongolia, having made sizeable contributions to that end since 1991;

Whereas in 1991, the United States (1) signed a bilateral trade agreement that restored normal trade relations with Mongolia; and (2) established a Peace Corps program in Mongolia that has had 869 total volunteers since 1991;

Whereas in 1999, the United States granted permanent normal trade relations status to Mongolia;

Whereas the Government of Mongolia has increasingly participated in the International Monetary Fund, the World Bank, the Asian Development Bank, and the European Bank for Reconstruction and Development, among other international organizations;

Whereas in 2007, the House Democracy Partnership began a program to provide parliamentary assistance to the State Great Hural, the Parliament of Mongolia, to promote transparency, legislative independence, access to information and government oversight;

Whereas on May 24, 2009, the people of Mongolia completed the country's fourth free, fair, and peaceful democratic election, which resulted in the election of opposition Democratic Party candidate Tsakhiagiin Elbegdorj;

Whereas in July 2011, Mongolia will assume the two-year chairmanship of the Community of Democracies;

Whereas in 2013, Mongolia will host the Seventh Ministerial Meeting of the Community of Democracies in Ulaanbaatar;

Whereas the Government of Mongolia continues to work with the United States Government to combat global terrorism;

Whereas Mongolia deployed about 990 soldiers to Iraq from 2003 to 2008 and has 190 troops in Afghanistan;

Whereas in 2010, the Government of Mongolia deployed a United Nations Level II hospital in Darfur, Sudan;

Whereas the Government of Mongolia has actively promoted international peacekeeping efforts by sending soldiers (1) to protect the Special Court of Sierra Leone; (2) to support the North Atlantic Treaty Organization in Kosovo; and (3) to support United Nations missions in several African countries;

Whereas the Government of Mongolia has built a successful partnership since 2003 with the Alaska National Guard that includes humanitarian and peacekeeping exercises and efforts;

Whereas the United States and the Government of Mongolia share a common interest in promoting peace and stability in Northeast Asia and Central Asia;

Whereas in 1991 and 1992, the Government of Mongolia signed denuclearization agreements committing Mongolia to remain a nuclear weapons–free state;

Whereas in 2010, Mongolia became the Chair of the Board of Governors of the International Atomic Energy Agency;

Whereas in 2010, the United States and Mongolia signed a Memorandum of Understanding to promote cooperation on the peaceful use of civil nuclear energy;

Whereas the National Security Administration and the Nuclear Energy Agency of the Government of Mongolia successfully completed training on response mechanisms to potential terrorist attacks;

Whereas between 1991 and 2011, the United States Government granted assistance to Mongolia (1) to advance the legal and regulatory environment for business and financial markets, including the mining sector; (2) to promote the reduction of greenhouse gas emissions; and (3) to support good governance programming;

Whereas in 2007, the Millennium Challenge Corporation signed an agreement with Mongolia to promote sustainable economic growth and to reduce poverty by focusing on property rights, vocational education, health, transportation, energy and the environment;

Whereas Mongolia's plan to enhance its rail infrastructure promises to diversify its trading and investment partners, to open up new markets for its mineral exports, and to position Mongolia as a bridge between Asia and Europe;

Whereas the United States has assisted Mongolia's efforts (1) to address the effects of the global economic crisis; (2) to promote sound economic, trade and energy policy, with particular attention to the banking and mining sectors; (3) to facilitate commercial law development; and (4) to further activities with Mongolia's peacekeeping forces and military;

Whereas in January 2010 (1) the United States Government and the Government of Mongolia agreed to promote greater academic exchange opportunities; (2) the Mongolian Ministry of Education, Culture and Science pledged to financially support the U.S.-Mongolia Fulbright Program; and (3) the United States Department of State announced its intention to increase its base allocation for the U.S.-Mongolia Fulbright Program in fiscal year 2010;

Whereas in 2011, Mongolia is celebrating the 100 year anniversary of its independence;

Whereas on June 16, 2011, President Elbegdorj, during a working visit to the United States, is scheduled to meet with President Barack Obama, Congressional leaders, academics, and representatives of the business community;

Whereas in late 2011, Vice President Joseph Biden is scheduled to travel to Mongolia to highlight our shared interests and values;

Now therefore be it resolved that it is the sense of the Senate that:

(1) Mongolian President Tsakhiagiin Elbegdorj's historic visit to Washington, DC, cements the growing friendship between the government and people of the United States and Mongolia;

(2) The continued commitment of the Mongolian people and the Government of Mongolia to advancing democratic reforms, strengthening transparency, and the rule of law, and protecting investment deserves acknowledgement and celebration;

(3) The United States Government should (a) continue to promote economic cooperation; and (b) consider next steps in securing increased investment and trade to promote prosperity for both countries;

(4) The United States Government should continue to support the Government of Mongolia as it works with the International Monetary Fund, the World Bank, the Asian Development Bank, and the European Bank for Reconstruction and Development to improve its economic system and accelerate development; and

(5) The United States Government should continue to expand upon existing academic, cultural and other people-to-people exchanges with Mongolia.

Major Sources and Further Reading

Addleton, Jonathan. 2012. Mongolia and the United States, a Long Way in a Short Time. *Ambassadors Review*, Spring.

———. 2010. Three of a Kind: Reflections on the Triad Tradition in Mongolia. *GUNU*, Winter.

Allen, Thomas B. 1985. Time Catches Up with Mongolia. *National Geographic*, February.

Andrews, Roy Chapman. 1933. Explorations in the Gobi Desert. *National Geographic*, June.

Angus, Colin. 2003. *Lost in Mongolia*. New York: Broadway Books.

Asia Society. 2005. *US-Mongolian Relations: History and Future Prospects*. Washington, DC: Asia Society.

Atwood, Christopher. 2004. *Encyclopedia of Mongolia and the Mongol Empire*. New York: Facts on File.

Baabar, Bat-erdene Batbayar. 1999. *History of Mongolia*. Cambridge, UK: White Horse Press.

Baatar, Tsendiin. 2001. *The Chinggis Heritage in the USA: Mongolian Americans in the 20th Century*. Ulaanbaatar: Mongolian Academy of Sciences.

Batsaikhan, Emgent Ookhnoi. 2009. *Bogdo Jebtsundamba Khutuktu: The Last King of Mongolia*. Ulaanbaatar: Mongolian Academy of Sciences.

Becker, Jasper. 1992. *Mongolia: Travels in an Untamed Land*. London: Hodder and Stoughton.

Campi, Alicia. 2006. American Christian Missionaries in Mongolia in the Early 20th Century and Their Impact on U.S. Government Policies. In *Christianity and Mongolia,* ed. Gaby Bamana. Ulaanbaatar: Antoon Mostaert Mongolian Study Center.

———, and R. Basan. 2009. *The Impact of China and Russia on United States–Mongolian Relations in the Twentieth Century*. Lampeter, UK: Edwin Mellen Press.

Colvin, John. 1991. *Twice around the World*. London: Leo Cooper.

Croner, Don. 2010. *Travels in Northern Mongolia*. Ulaanbaatar: Polar Star Books.

Davis, Matthew. 2010. *When Things Get Dark: A Mongolian Winter's Tale*. New York: St. Martin's Press.

Dierkes, Julian, ed. 2012. *Change in Democratic Mongolia: Social Relations, Health, Mobile Pastoralism and Mining*. Leiden: E. J. Brill.

Douglas, William O. 1962. Journey to Outer Mongolia. *National Geographic*. March.

Drompp, Michael R., ed. 2007. *The Memoir of Frans August Larson*. Bloomington, IN: Mongolia Society Special Papers Issue Sixteen.

Dumbaugh, Kerry, and Wayne M. Morrison. 2009. *Mongolia and U.S. Policy: Political and Economic Relations*. Washington, DC: Congressional Research Service, June 18.

Finch, Christopher. 1999. *Mongolia's Wild Heritage*. Boulder, CO: Avery Press.

Fish, M. S. 1998. Mongolia: Democracy without Prerequisites. *Journal of Democracy*, July.

Fitzhugh, William W. 2005. *The Deer Stone Project: Anthropological Studies in Mongolia, 2002–2004*. Washington, DC: Smithsonian Institution.

Freeman, Patrick J., and Alexei Kral. 2007. Ulaanbaatar: Modern Nomads and Vast Horizons Mark U.S. "Neighbor." *State Magazine*, June.

Gallenkamp, Charles. 2001. *Dragon Hunter: Roy Chapman Andrews and the Central Asiatic Expeditions*. New York: Viking.

Ganbold, G., ed. 2010. *Foreign Coins, Banknotes and Other Media of Exchange Used in Mongolia*. Ulaanbaatar: Munkhiin Useg Group.

Gilmour, Rev. James. Undated. *Among the Mongols*. London: Religious Tract Society.

Goldstein, Melvyn C., and Cynthia M. Beall. 1994. *The Changing World of Mongolia's Nomads*. Hong Kong: Odyssey.

Hangin, John Gombojab, ed. 1998. *Mongolian Folklore*. Bloomington, IN: Mongolia Society.

Hasenkopf, Christa. 2012. Clearing the Air. *World Policy Journal*, Spring.

Hibbert, Reginald and Ann. 2005. *Letters from Mongolia*. London: Radcliffe Press.

Hopkirk, Peter. 1984. *Setting the East Ablaze*. New York and London: W. W. Norton.

Jeffries, Ian. 2007. *Mongolia: A Guide to Economic and Political Developments*. New York: Routledge.

Kaplan, Robert. 2004. The Man Who Would be Khan. *Atlantic Monthly*, March.

Khutagt, Diluv. 2009. *The Diluv Khutagt of Mongolia: Political Memoirs and Autobiography of a Buddhist Reincarnation*. Ulaanbaatar: Polar Star Books.

Knauft, Bruce M., and Richard Taupier, eds. 2012. *Mongolians after Socialism: Politics, Economy, Religion*. Ulaanbaatar: Admon.

Knox, Thomas W. 1868. A Journey through Mongolia. *Galaxy*, August.

Kohn, Michael. 2006. *Dateline Mongolia: An American Journalist in Nomad's Land*. Berkeley, CA: RDR Books.

———. 2006. *Lama of the Gobi*. Ulaanbaatar: Maitri Books.

Lake, Joseph. 1992. Frontier Embassy. *Foreign Service Journal*, December.

Larson, Frans August. 1930. *Duke of Mongolia*. Boston: Little, Brown and Company.

Lattimore, Owen. 1942. *Mongol Journeys*. London: Travel Book Club.

. 2009. *The Diluv Khutagt of Mongolia*. Ulaanbaatar: Polar Star Books.

Man, John. 1997. *Gobi: Tracking the Desert*. New Haven and London: Yale University Press.

Mann, Steve. 1989. Making It in Mongolia. *State Magazine*, March.

Matthiessen, Peter. 2001. *The Birds of Heaven: Travels with Cranes*. Vancouver: Greystone Books.

Mendee, Jargalsaikhan. 2007. *Mongolia's Peacekeeping Commitment: Training, Deployment and Evolution of Field Information Capabilities*. Washington, DC: National Defense Intelligence College Discussion Paper Number Fifteen.

Montagu, Ivor. 1956. *Land of Blue Sky*. London: Dennis Dobson.

Munkh-Amgalan, Yumjiriin. 2003–2004. American Literature in Mongolian Textbooks. *Mongolian Studies*, XXVI.

Murphy, David. 2002. Mongolia's Bank Reformer. *Far Eastern Economic Review*, July 18.

Nyamdorj, Gonchigdorj. 2011. *Back to Baghdad*. Ulaanbaatar: Mongolian Armed Forces Newspaper.

Palmer, James. 2009. *The Bloody White Baron*. New York: Basic Books.

Prohl, Werner, and Luvsandendev Sumati. Undated. *Voters' Choices: People's Perceptions of Mongolia's Political and Economic Transition as Reflected in Opinion Polls from 1995 to 2007*. Ulaanbaatar: publisher not indicated.

Raymond, Janice. 2010. *Mongolian Proverbs*. San Diego: Alethinos Books.

Reinert, Erik. 2004. Globalization in the Periphery as a Morgenthau Plan: The Underdevelopment of Mongolia in the 1990s. In *Globalization, Economic Development and Inequality: An Alternative Perspective*, ed. Erik Reinert. Cheltenham, UK: Edward Elgar.

Roerich, Nicholas. 2009. *Heart of Asia*. Ulaanbaatar: Polar Star Books.

Rossabi, Morris. 2005. *Modern Mongolia: From Khans to Commissars to Capitalists*. Berkeley and Los Angeles: University of California Press.

Sabloff, Paula L., ed. 2001. *Modern Mongolia: Reclaiming Genghis Khan*. Philadelphia: University of Pennsylvania Museum of Archeology and Anthropology.

Sanday, Shagdariin, and Harry H. Kendall. 2000. *Poisoned Arrows: The Stalin-Choibalsan Mongolian Massacres, 1921–1941*. Boulder, CO: Westview.

Sanders, Alan J. K. 2010. *Historical Dictionary of Mongolia*. Plymouth, UK: Scarecrow Press.

Sinor, Denis. 2007. A Mongolian Diplomatic Approach to the United States Written in 1952. *Mongolian Studies*, XXIX.

Stewart, Stanley. 2002. *In the Empire of Genghis Khan*. Guilford, CT: Lyon's Press.

Thayer, Helen. 2007. *Walking the Gobi*. Seattle, WA: Mountaineers Books.

Tolme, Andre. 2009. *I Golfed across Mongolia*. New York: Thunder's Mouth Press.

Tubat, Tsagaan, et al. 2011. *Deer Stones of the Jargalantyn Am*. Ulaanbaatar: National Museum of Mongolia.

Uranchimeg, Ts., ed. Undated. *The Khan Bank Collection of Mongolian Contemporary Art*. Ulaanbaatar: Khan Bank.

U.S. Agency for International Development. 2003. *USAID Country Strategic Plan for Mongolia, 2004–2008*. Ulaanbaatar: USAID/Mongolia.

———. 2003. *Internal Assessment and Evaluation: USAID Country Strategic Plan for Mongolia, 1998–2003*. Ulaanbaatar: USAID/Mongolia.

Wachman, Alan. 2012. Mongolia: Growth, Democracy and Two Wary Neighbors. Interview with Allen Wagner. *National Bureau of Asian Research*, May.

Wallace, Henry A. Undated. *Soviet Asia Mission*. New York: Reynal and Hitchcock Publishers.

Weatherford, Jack. 2004. *Genghis Khan and the Making of the Modern World*. New York: Crown Publishers.

———. 2010. *The Secret History of the Mongol Queens*. New York: Crown Publishers.

Wickham-Smith, Simon, trans. 2008. *An Anthology of Mongolian Literature*. Ulaanbaatar: Mongolian Academy of Culture and Poetry.

Acknowledgments

This book is based on contributions and support from many people, including a number of American officials and Mongolian staff who either served or are currently serving at the US Embassy in Ulaanbaatar: Allyson Algeo, Alissa Bibb, Charles Bouldin, Philip Cargile, Andrew Covington, Rick Donovan, Onder Durmas, George Economides, Uyanga Erdenebold, Tim Feeney, Jeff Goodson, Mendsaikhan Hasbaatar, Chuck Howell, Burak Inanc, Jonathan Lau, Peggy Matsuya, Marissa Maurer, Ellen Paquette, Lisa Powers, Tina Puntsag, Dan Rakove, Robert Reid, Michael Richmond, Susan Russell, Luvsanjav Sambuu, Vinny Spera, "Tumi" Tumenbayar, Lisa Vining, Michael Vining, David Wyche, and Otgon Yondon, among many others. I also want to pay special tribute to the two deputy chiefs of mission with whom I served in Ulaanbaatar, Nick Hill and Kathleen Morenski. Both of them made my job far easier, and I will always be grateful for their many contributions during my own tenure in Mongolia between November 2009 and July 2012.

Several former US ambassadors who served previously in Mongolia provided recollections and made recommendations on portions of the text. They include Mark Minton, Pamela Slutz, John Dinger, Al La Porta, Joseph Lake (the first resident US ambassador in Mongolia), and Richard Williams (the first US ambassador accredited to Mongolia). The Foreign Affairs Oral History Collection of the Association for Diplomatic Studies and Training (ADST), available on the Web sites of ADST and the Library of Congress, also proved very helpful. The collection includes long interviews with Ambassador Lake and Ambassador La Porta that touch at length on Mongolia. Some quotations in the text of this book are based on those interviews.

Defense Attaché Tom Wilhelm, whose role in working with the Mongolian military during the early 2000s is described at length in Robert D. Kaplan's "The Man Who Would Be Khan" (*Atlantic Monthly*, March 2004), provided encouragement as well as helpful comments on the chapter related to security relations between the United States and Mongolia. Layton Croft, a former Peace Corps volunteer, NGO worker, Asia Foundation country director, and mining company executive in Mongolia, contributed a number of useful suggestions, especially on the section summarizing various Peace Corps programs. Chris Finch, founding executive director of the Open Society Forum in Mongolia, provided several useful comments, especially on the chapter focused on democracy.

The late Professor Alan Wachman of the Fletcher School of Law and Diplomacy at Tufts University made several specific suggestions. His all too early death in June 2012 deprives those who follow Mongolia of a calm, incisive, prescient, and above all balanced view of Mongolian foreign policy and the role that Mongolia plays in the region and beyond. Lawyer Michael Aldrich, author of several books—including *Vanishing Beijing* (Hong Kong University Press, 2006) and *The Perfumed Palace* (Garnet Publishing, 2010)—also offered important encouragement and advice throughout the project. Longtime friend and USAID colleague Chris Brown gave additional support, as did Robin Charpentier, former country director of the American Center for Mongolian Studies in Ulaanbaatar.

Let me also thank both Kenneth L. Brown, president of the Association for Diplomatic Studies and Training (ADST) in Arlington, Virginia, and Margery Boichel Thompson, ADST's publishing director and series editor, for their advice and support. Ambassador Brown offered encouragement at an especially critical time, while Margery Thompson provided help with the manuscript and the search for a publisher and endorsed the decision to include this book in ADST's continuing series on "Diplomats and Diplomacy." Thanks also to Kevin Brazda for help in formatting the final manuscript during his internship at ADST.

Finally, I must thank Tsogtbaatar, who during my tenure as United States ambassador to Mongolia served first as Mongolian State Secretary for Foreign Affairs and Trade and later as Mongolia's Minister for Nature, Tourism and the Environment. In early 2011 he encouraged me to "do something" to help mark the 25th anniversary of US-Mongolian diplomatic relations in 2012. I hope that this book meets his expectations!

Much of the documentation contained in this volume relies on personal memories along with newspaper accounts and unpublished reports, photographs, e-mails, Web sites, and other less traditional source material. Some published work—most of it listed in the bibliography—also proved invaluable.

It is important to acknowledge most notably the pioneering work by Alicia Campi and R. Baasan, *The Impact of China and Russia on United States–Mongolian Political Relations in the Twentieth Century* (Edwin Mellen Press, 2009). No doubt future books will explore in still greater depth many facets of US-Mongolian relations as they continue to develop over time. However, this heavily footnoted work stands out for the depth and breadth of its research, as well as its extensive use of archival material found in both the United States and Mongolia, material that otherwise would not be available to the general public. Moreover, Alicia Campi kindly read the first draft of this manuscript, making a number of important suggestions that have been incorporated into the text and most definitely improve it.

I also want to acknowledge important encouragement from Jack Weatherford, author of *Genghis Khan and the Making of the Modern World* (Crown Publishers, 2004). In each of the three summers that I spent in Ulaanbaatar as ambassador, Jack and his wife Walker gave me inspiration as well as a refuge in their apartment in downtown Ulaanbaatar near the State Department store, providing many welcome and enjoyable opportunities to talk about all things Mongolian. Indeed, it is doubtful that this book would ever have been completed or published without their continued encouragement and support.

In addition, I want to express my personal appreciation to Erdenebold Sukhbaatar, founder and president of the Jack Weatherford Foundation, based in Ulaanbaatar. In particular, it was Erdenebold through the Weatherford Foundation that published the Mongolian edition of an earlier version of this manuscript in May 2012, making it available to a Mongolian audience.

Finally, this book is dedicated to my wife Fiona, who for the last quarter century has accompanied and supported me on Foreign Service assignments in virtually every corner of the world, including Belgium, Cambodia, Jordan, Kazakhstan, Pakistan, South Africa, Yemen, and Mongolia; and to our three children Iain, Cameron, and Catriona, who spent important portions of their childhoods living in Mongolia, accompanying me on numerous field trips, camping in some of the most remote parts of the country, and visiting places that are more usually seen in late night episodes on *National Geographic* and *Discovery Channel.* Families, though often stretched to the limit, are the true "heroes" of Foreign Service life. My own family certainly fits into that category—all too often having had to endure a frustrating bureaucracy, frequent moves, and occasional long separations. I will always remain grateful for their enduring love and support, a love and support that, literally, extends to the ends of the earth.

Index

About the Author

Jonathan S. Addleton served as a US Foreign Service officer in Mongolia twice, first as USAID mission director (2001–04) and then as ambassador (2009–12). Other assignments include development counselor at the US Mission to the European Union in Brussels; USAID mission director in Pakistan and Cambodia; and USAID program officer in Jordan, Kazakhstan, South Africa, and Yemen. He has written a number of articles on Asia as well as two previous books, *Undermining the Center* (Oxford University Press, 1992) and *Some Far and Distant Place* (University of Georgia Press, 1997). In July 2012, he was awarded the Polar Star, Mongolia's highest civilian honor conferred on foreign citizens, for his role in strengthening ties between the United States and Mongolia.